Star Kingdom: The Wonder of Chinese Astrology

Emily Mazanowski

Copyright 2022 by Emily Mazanowski

All Rights Reserved Ragtag Publishing.

Star Kingdom: The Wonder of Chinese Astrology Book | Chinese Ancient Civilizations and Chinese Zodiac Sign Book | Unique Astronomy Gifts and Astronomy Books | Chinese Zodiac Book

All rights reserved. No portion of this book may be reproduced, scanned, or distributed in any form without the written permission of the author, Emily Mazanowski

Table of Contents

Preface 1
Basics 5
Yin and Yang 7
Chinese Calendar 10
Measuring Months 11
Naming Months 12
Measuring Days 12
Measuring Weeks 13
Stems and Branches (Tiān Gān Dì Zhi, or Ganzhi) 14
The Chinese Vision of the Sky 19
Sān yuan (Three Enclosures) 20
Shijin (Four Directions) 23
The Five Element Theory 32
Five Elements Theory and the Chinese Zodiac 34
Traits of the Element Metal 36
Traits of the Element Water 38
Traits of the Element of Wood 40
Traits of the Element Fire 43
Traits of the Element Earth 45
The 12 Signs of the Zodiac 47
Credits: 113

Preface

Whenever I hear a story that has trickled down from ancient times, my curiosity is piqued about the culture behind the story. The imagery used is so creative and full of insights about the daily life of the ancient people! The little tidbits in the stories speak to the trained historian in me, and I happily spend a couple hours learning new things about ancient cultures. The original story becomes so much more interesting and complete when I have context.

This is what happened to me one day when I was looking for information on the personality aspects of the 12 Chinese zodiac animals. As a child, I always loved reading about which personality I was when the Chinese menu had the animals listed. I wanted to be a monkey because I thought they were cool; I'm a rabbit and thought that was lame.

What was supposed to be a simple thing for a work project drew me into an ancient world so full of imagination and complex relationships and star-filled kingdoms that the 'couple hours' I usually spent quickly turned into weeks! I just couldn't get a handle on how the whole intricate puzzle fit together so I kept researching it until I felt I could summarize it down. My uncle once told me that if you can't explain something so that a 5-year-old can understand it, you don't really understand it yourself.

This is my humble attempt at a summarization, but maybe not for 5-year-old level! I don't claim to be an expert in any way, shape, or form, and I do not live by this belief system myself. I mean no disrespect to anyone by my interpretation of the complex issues I researched.

These astrological views still influence a great deal of Chinese society; it would seem it is interwoven into every aspect of life. I had no idea when I started how deep into Chinese culture I would dive! I found it so fascinating that I wanted to share it. And so, this book was born.

My intention with this book is simply to share knowledge on an interesting subject in hopes that it inspires you to learn more about another culture. The main point of this book is to better understand how the 12-animal cycle came about and how it relates to temperaments. It's for those who find the personality aspect of astrology entertaining, but don't necessarily believe in the fortune-telling aspect.

For comparison's sake, the Chinese system is looked at next to the Western system quite often. The background on how these systems develop are fascinating! Links are provided throughout this short book for further reading should curiosity strike.

The Western Astrology school of thought follows a linear concept of time, so like a line that keeps going on and on and on. The Chinese system uses a 12-year cycle system that represents a cyclical concept of time, so everything continues on a path like a circle. Each year is represented by one of 12 animals in a cycle: in order, rat, ox, tiger, rabbit, dragon, snake, horse, sheep (or ram or goat), monkey, rooster, dog, and pig.

Personality descriptions have developed around the yearly animal signs (生肖 'Sheng Xiao', which literally means 'birth likeness'). There are detailed breakdowns of each animal in this book, as well as the 5 Elements, so get excited! Also included are high-quality charts and illustrations to help you further understand these concepts.

First thing's first: What is **your** animal sign? Check the chart on the next page (Figure 1), find your birth year, and there you go! You will also see which element is yours, and whether you are Yin or Yang. It's believed by some that people have different characters and destinies according to their birth year's zodiac sign and element.

Your element + whether you are Yin or Yang + the animal ruling the year in which you were born = profound influence on your life.

It's the animal that hides in your heart.

Once you know your animal, let's find out a little more about what that means. Why the twelve animals? Why the one-year span instead of the monthly time frame of the Western world? Let's dive in!

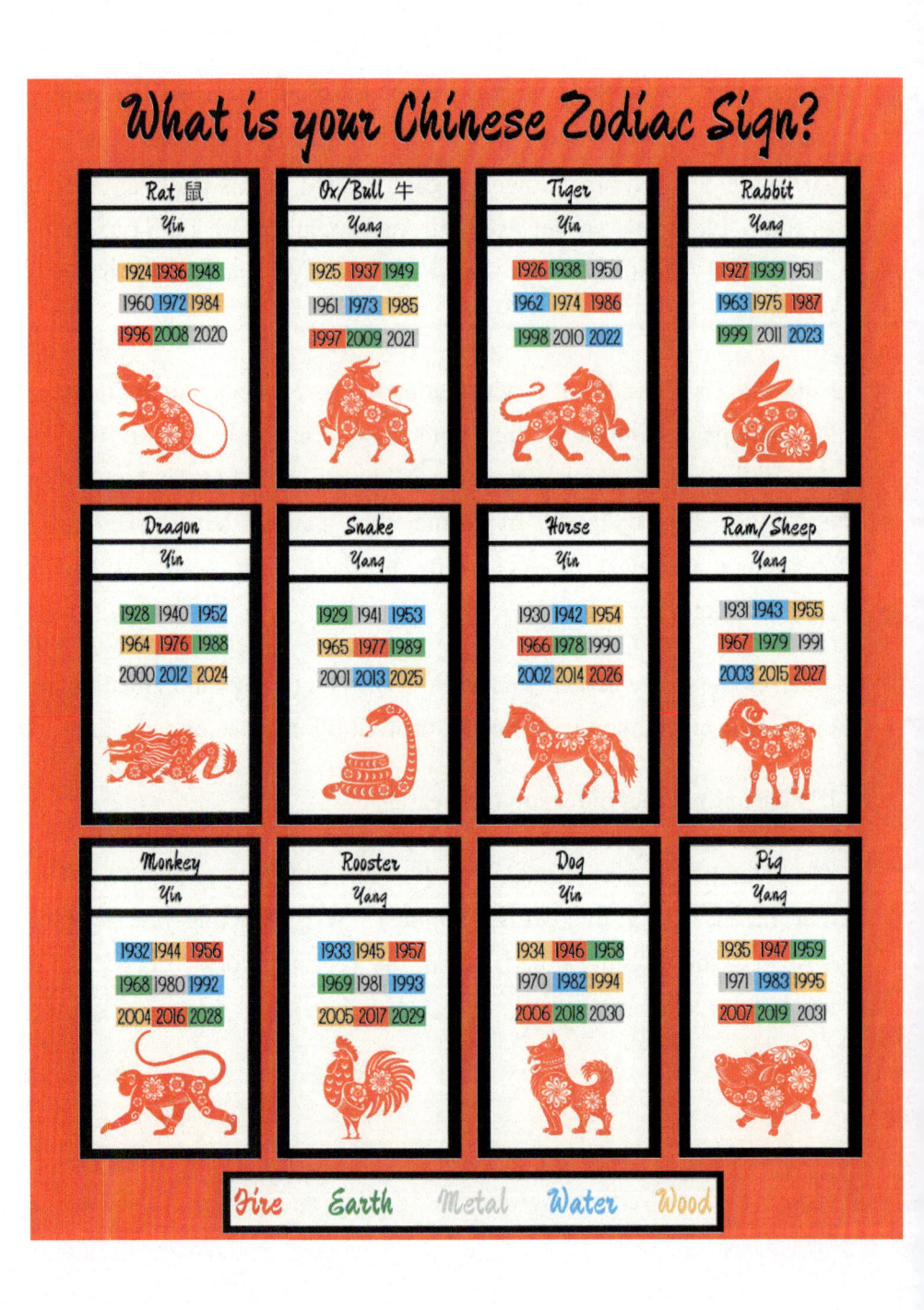

Figure 1

Basics

The ancient Chinese astrologers worked with little to no contact with those of the Greek world. This relative isolation means the constellations we know in the western world are unheard of in Chinese astrology; they have a system entirely their own. Chinese Astrology is concerned with nature and its traits, rhythms, and cycles. Thus, the signs progress year by year, whereas Western Astrology cycles monthly.

Though they all reside in the same hemisphere of stars, there are many more constellations in the Chinese sky (283) than in the Western sky (88); the Chinese versions are in smaller groups with fewer stars. The whole sky is viewed as a reflection of the Chinese nation on Earth, like a still lake reflecting the sky. Only this time, the sky is the still lake reflecting the Earth.

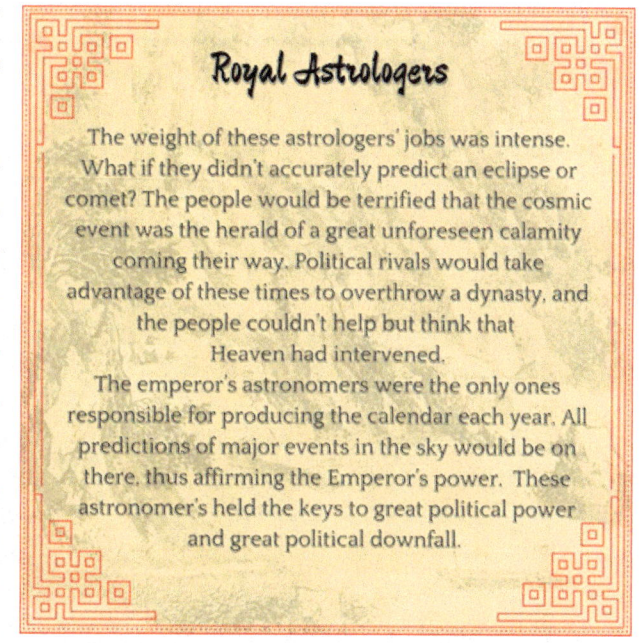

> **Royal Astrologers**
>
> The weight of these astrologers' jobs was intense. What if they didn't accurately predict an eclipse or comet? The people would be terrified that the cosmic event was the herald of a great unforeseen calamity coming their way. Political rivals would take advantage of these times to overthrow a dynasty, and the people couldn't help but think that Heaven had intervened.
>
> The emperor's astronomers were the only ones responsible for producing the calendar each year. All predictions of major events in the sky would be on there, thus affirming the Emperor's power. These astronomer's held the keys to great political power and great political downfall.

The ancient Chinese astrologers believed that events in the sky directly affected events on earth. The emperor was believed to be the Son of Heaven who had been given the Mandate, or right to rule, by Heaven itself. If you're the Son of Heaven, you're going to understand the Heavens, right? Otherwise, how could you protect your people from the calamities the sky predicted?

You can see how his greatest interest would be with making sure the heavens were on his side so that his reign was deemed legitimate. His astronomers were therefore expected to watch the sky very carefully, and woe to them if they didn't accurately translate the phenomena of the skies. They kept fastidious records of the movements of the stars and planets, recording events such as Halley's comet and various eclipses of the sun and moon.

To the Chinese, the planets do not hold as much importance as the stars and they are named with the five Chinese elements:

Mars with fire 火星 'fire star'

Jupiter with wood 木星

Venus with metal 金星

Mercury with water 水星

Saturn with earth 土星

The apparent color and shape of the planets was used to predict important events; for example if Saturn appears red then calamity is at hand. This is true for the Western astronomy of that time as well.

Yin and Yang

The topic of Yin and Yang is one that pervades every area of Chinese culture. Before we go any further into the astronomy behind the 12 Zodiac animals, let's look at what Yin and Yang means beyond the famous YinYang symbol.

The various permutations of these 2 essential forces in nature and the quest to achieve balance is an essentially Oriental viewpoint. Not just in nature are these forces at work but also in places, organizations, events, and humanity itself. The quest is to get both Yin and Yang forces to operate together in harmony rather than opposing or canceling each other out. They form the basis of many Far Eastern traditions and other influences such as Feng Shui.

The person is Yin or Yang, which is determined by the year of their birth based on the Chinese calendar, as you saw on Figure 1 which determined your Zodiac sign.

Yin

Negative	Decrease
Passive	Decline
Female	Shrinking

Heavenly Stems:
Yi, Ding, Ji, Xin, Gui

Earthly Branches:
Chou, Mao, Si, Wei, You, Hai
(Ox, Rabbit, Snake, Sheep, Rooster, Pig)

If the year ends in 1 it is Yin Metal.
If the year ends in 3 it is Yin Water.
If the year ends in 5 it is Yin Wood.
If the year ends in 7 it is Yin Fire.
If the year ends in 9 it is Yin Earth.

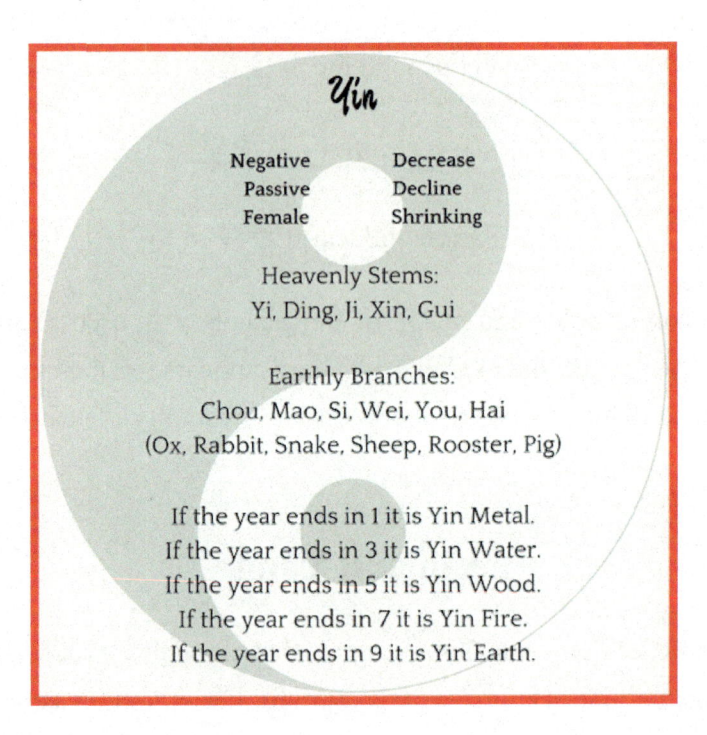

Figure 2

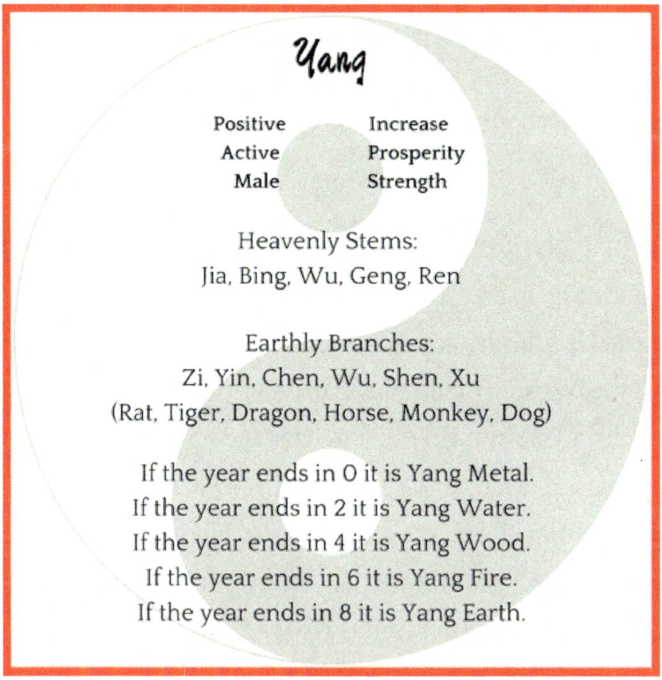

Yang

Positive   Increase
Active   Prosperity
Male   Strength

Heavenly Stems:
Jia, Bing, Wu, Geng, Ren

Earthly Branches:
Zi, Yin, Chen, Wu, Shen, Xu
(Rat, Tiger, Dragon, Horse, Monkey, Dog)

If the year ends in 0 it is Yang Metal.
If the year ends in 2 it is Yang Water.
If the year ends in 4 it is Yang Wood.
If the year ends in 6 it is Yang Fire.
If the year ends in 8 it is Yang Earth.

Figure 3

Now that we understand that concept a little better, let's look at the Chinese Calendar system.

Chinese Calendar

The Chinese calendar is based on lunar cycles or phases of the moon.

China exclusively followed a lunar calendar in determining the times of planting, harvesting, and festival occasions until adopting the Western Gregorian calendar in 1911. Though today people in China use the Western calendar for most practical matters of daily life, the old system still serves as the basis for determining numerous seasonal holidays. Many Chinese calendars today will print both the solar dates and the Chinese lunar dates. Interestingly, the same (or a very similar lunar calendar) is also used by other East Asian countries including Korea, Vietnam, Thailand, and Japan.

It is important to note that the Chinese New Year (the Spring Festival) falls on a different day from the Western New Year. Since its based off the moon's movement, the month with its first day nearest the Beginning of Spring is the first lunar month, and that determines when the Spring Festival (and the Chinese New Year) is held. This varies between January 20th and February 20th.

Measuring Months

As mentioned before, the calendar was also vital to the success of farming at the time, as the predictions were used to predict the best times to plant and harvest crops. Noting the ever-changing position of the moon, the stars, and the planets were key to accurately predicting the change of seasons and flow of the tides for all ancient cultures.

In Western astrology importance is given to the Zodiac, which are the twelve constellations that the *Sun* moves through during the year.

By contrast, the Chinese concentrated on 28 'Mansions' (*xiu* or sù 宿) that mark the latitudes the *Moon* crosses during its monthly journey around Earth; they serve to track the Moon's progress. So, a Mansion is what we would know of as a constellation and was integral to the Chinese calendar.

Each time the moon moves into a line with the earth and the sun, a new month begins. No Chinese month has a set number of days, so one year a month could have 29 days and the next year it would have 30 days depending on the moon's progress. When the full moon appears, it is the middle of the month. As a new moon comes roughly every 29½ days, Chinese calendar months always have 29 or 30 days. This translates into there being 12 – 13 months in a lunar year. A 13th month was added every 3 years to get things back in line with what is known as 'the tropical year'. Basically, this made sure the lunar calendar matched up with the solar calendar.

This system has the practical benefit that you can tell the day of the month by looking at the current location of the moon against the stars. The Western solar zodiac system gives only a vague idea of the current month, as you cannot see the constellation that the sun is apparently in front of.

Naming Months

Month Number	"Approximate" Gregorian Dates	Phenological Name	Earthly Branch	Common Name
1	21 January – 20 February	陬月: zōuyuè: 'corner month'	寅月: yínyuè: 'tiger month'	正月: zhēngyuè: 'first month'
2	20 February – 21 March	杏月: xìngyuè: 'apricot month'	卯月: mǎoyuè: 'rabbit month'	二月: èryuè: 'second month'
3	21 March – 20 April	桃月: táoyuè: 'peach month'	辰月: chényuè: 'dragon month'	三月: sānyuè: 'third month'
4	20 April – 21 May	梅月: méiyuè: 'plum month'	巳月: sìyuè: 'snake month'	四月: sìyuè: 'fourth month'
5	21 May – 21 June	榴月: liúyuè: 'pomegranate month'	午月: wǔyuè: 'horse month'	五月: wǔyuè: 'fifth month'
6	21 June – 23 July	荷月: héyuè: 'lotus month'	未月: wèiyuè: 'goat month'	六月: liùyuè: 'sixth month'
7	23 July – 23 August	蘭月, 兰月: lányuè: 'orchid month'	申月: shēnyuè: 'monkey month'	七月: qīyuè: 'seventh month'
8	23 August – 23 September	桂月: guìyuè: 'osmanthus month'	酉月: yǒuyuè: 'rooster month'	八月: bāyuè: 'eighth month'
9	23 September – 23 October	菊月: júyuè: 'chrysanthemum month'	戌月: xūyuè: 'dog month'	九月: jiǔyuè: 'ninth month'
10	23 October – 22 November	露月: lùyuè: 'dew month'	亥月: hàiyuè: 'pig month'	十月: shíyuè: 'tenth month'
11	22 November – 22 December	冬月: dōngyuè: 'winter month' 葭月: jiāyuè: 'reed month'	子月: zǐyuè: 'rat month'	冬月: dōngyuè: 'eleventh month'
12	22 December – 21 January	冰月: bīngyuè: 'ice month'	丑月: chǒuyuè: 'ox month'	臘月, 腊月: làyuè: 'end-of-year month'

Lunar months were originally named according to natural phenomena. Current naming conventions use numbers as the month names. Every month is also associated with one of the twelve Earthly Branches.

Measuring Days

China has used the Western hour-minute-second system to divide the day since the Qing dynasty.

The days of the month are always written with two characters and numbered beginning with 1. Days one to 10 are written with the day's numeral, preceded by the character *Chū* (初); *Chūyī* (初一) is the first day of the month, and *Chūshí* (初十) the 10th. Days 11 to 20 are written as regular Chinese numerals; *Shíwǔ* (十五) is the 15th day of the month, and *Èrshí* (二十) the 20th. Days 21 to 29 are written with the character *Niàn* (廿) before the characters one through nine; *Niànsān* (廿三), for example, is the 23rd day of the month. Day 30 (as applicable) is written as the numeral *Sānshí* (三十).

Because astronomical observation determines month length, dates on the calendar correspond to moon phases. The first day of each month is the new moon. On the seventh or eighth day of each month, the first-quarter moon is visible in the afternoon and early evening. On the 15th or 16th day of the month the full moon is visible all night long. On the 22nd or 23rd day of each month, the last-quarter moon is visible late at night and in the morning.

Measuring Weeks

As early as the Bronze-Age Xia dynasty, days were grouped into nine- or ten-day weeks known as *xún* (旬). Months consisted of three *xún*. The first 10 days were the *early xún* (上旬), the middle 10 the *mid xún* (中旬), and the last nine (or 10) days were the *late xún* (下旬).

- The structure of *xún* led to public holidays every five or ten days. During the Han dynasty, officials were legally required to rest every five days (twice a *xún*, or 5–6 times a month). The name of these breaks became *huan* (澣; 浣, "wash"…as in hair and body wash day).

Grouping days into sets of ten is still used today in referring to specific natural events. "Three Fu" (三伏), a 29–30-day period which is the hottest of the year, reflects its three-*xún* length.

The seven-day week was adopted from the Hellenistic system by the 4th century CE, and this is the most-used system in modern China.

Stems and Branches (Tiān Gān Dì Zhi, or Ganzhi)

To help them keep track of passing time, the Ten Heavenly Stems (*Gan*) and Twelve Earthly Branches (*Zhi*) were created. The Heavenly stems reflect the energy of Heaven, and the Earthly Branches represent the energy of the Earth. The *Ganzhi* (Stem-Branch) combination was developed in the second millennium BC, during the Shang era. Thus it is a fairly "new" way to mark time. The Earthly Branches are today used with the Heavenly Stems in the current version of the "traditional Chinese calendar" and in Taoism.

The Ten Heavenly Stems were created based on the Chinese myth that the Earth had ten suns. The people of the Shang Dynasty believed that there were ten suns, each of which appeared in order in a ten-day cycle. The Heavenly Stems were the names of the ten suns. These 10 Heavenly Stems provided the names of the days of the week. They are: Jia, Yi, Bing, Ding, Wu, Ji, Geng, Xin, Ren and Gui.

While they have this practical use of naming days, there is also a spiritual aspect that relates to our humanity. This description illustrates what the Heavenly Stems might say about themselves:

"We are the Heavenly Stems because we are the Qi [energy] from Heaven. We are your Good, your Bad and your Ugly. We can make you rich and wealthy instantly. And we can also destroy your entire life. We are your events, your outcomes and the successes and failures in life. We demonstrate to the world your life, and we make it obvious to others when the time is right. We are different from the Branches because we are not concerned about your feelings. You cannot hide us, but you can only control us by understanding our strengths and weaknesses." [Extracted from the book "The Correct Way of Understanding a Person's Destiny" by Benson Yeo].

In other words, the Heavenly Stems are the outward appearance of a person. They are what the person projects for people to see: character, outlook, events, and relationships that are obvious to those around him.

Initially, the stems were created to count the DAY only. For example, the 1st day is 甲 (Jia), 2nd day is 乙(Yi), the 10th day is 癸 (Gia) and the 11th goes back to 甲 (Jia) and so on. Every 10-day cycle is called Xún. Stems are still being used in the Chinese community today. 甲 (Jia) is used to refer to the best class in school or the highest-quality trading goods. Second best is 乙(Yi) and so on.

The Twelve Earthly Branches are the names of the months: Zi, Chou, Yin, Mao, Chen, Si, Wu, Wei, Shen, You, Xu and Hai.

During this ancient time in history, only the elite could read and write, so animals were used to symbolize each of the Twelve Earthly Branches. In other words:

Rat, Ox, Tiger, Rabbit, Dragon, Snake, Horse, Sheep (or ram or goat), Monkey, Rooster, Dog, and Pig.

The Zodiac was developed from these animal representations of the months. It's important to note that the Chinese words for these animals are NOT the same as the names of the months. This can be confusing, but the chart on the next page can help.

Let's hear again from Benson Yeo on what the Branches might say about themselves:

"We are your feeling and we are your hidden secrets. We take orders from Heaven (Stems). We are the creator of your character. We represent your house, your body, your potential illness and your hidden agenda. We are in hiding and when we receive orders from Heaven, your secrets will be revealed. We prefer to be still but sometimes moving or clashing us is a good sign. We can give you a sudden shock of surprise when we are being clashed or combined. Your feelings of happiness and sadness will largely depend on us because we can control it. If you can understand us, you can manage your feelings and be well prepared." [Extracted from the book "The Correct Way of Understanding a Person's Destiny" by Benson Yeo].

So, the Branches represent a person's feelings, thoughts, and intentions: that which is not obviously seen by those around you.

Any given Stem or Branch also contains the energy of one of the five elements. The way these interact with each other form the basis of the time tracking system of the Chinese. The *GanZhi* and the way they interact with each other, along with Yin and Yang, is a complicated dance that denotes the hours, days, months, and years.

The chart on the previous page shows how the 12 Earthly Branches form the name of the hours. The 24-hour period is broken down into 12, 2-hour periods, each with the name of one of the Earthly Branches. You can also see elements associated with the year, the season it occurs in, and how the Zodiac name differs from the year name. The Stems are listed at the bottom with element colors.

A 60-year cycle is formed by combining the ten Heavenly Stems, twelve Earthly Branches, and five elements (discussed in the next section) in a pattern. For example, the Wood Rat is ranked first in the 60-year Chinese zodiac-element cycle. 12 years later produces the Fire Rats, then Earth Rats, Metal (Gold) Rats, and Water Rats. It's the same for each of the other Zodiac signs and their Elements.

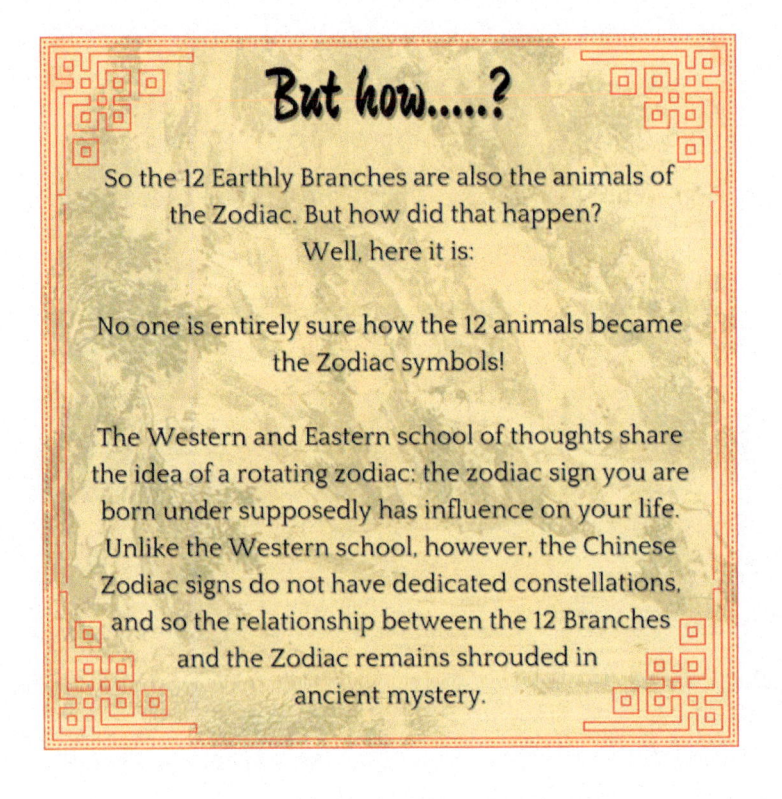

But how......?

So the 12 Earthly Branches are also the animals of the Zodiac. But how did that happen?
Well, here it is:

No one is entirely sure how the 12 animals became the Zodiac symbols!

The Western and Eastern school of thoughts share the idea of a rotating zodiac: the zodiac sign you are born under supposedly has influence on your life. Unlike the Western school, however, the Chinese Zodiac signs do not have dedicated constellations, and so the relationship between the 12 Branches and the Zodiac remains shrouded in ancient mystery.

Chinese astrology asserts that personality, luck, and destiny are determined by both Zodiac sign (animal) *and* 12-year cycle element. It goes much deeper into birth hours by practitioners of the divination aspect of these beliefs. The hour of your birth assigns your 'secret animal' and is the true sign upon which your personality is based. The hour itself is not based on local time but mapped according to the sun's location and can only be done by a professional in the field.

The Chinese Vision of the Sky

The Chinese sky was divided into five great regions or palaces called *gong* 宫. These were equated with the directions north, south, east, and west and also with a middle region. Each of the four directions is represented by an animal and a color. These four directions, or *shijin*, each contain seven of the twenty-eight mansions, and together with the central region of the sky make up what are known as the five cardinal points.

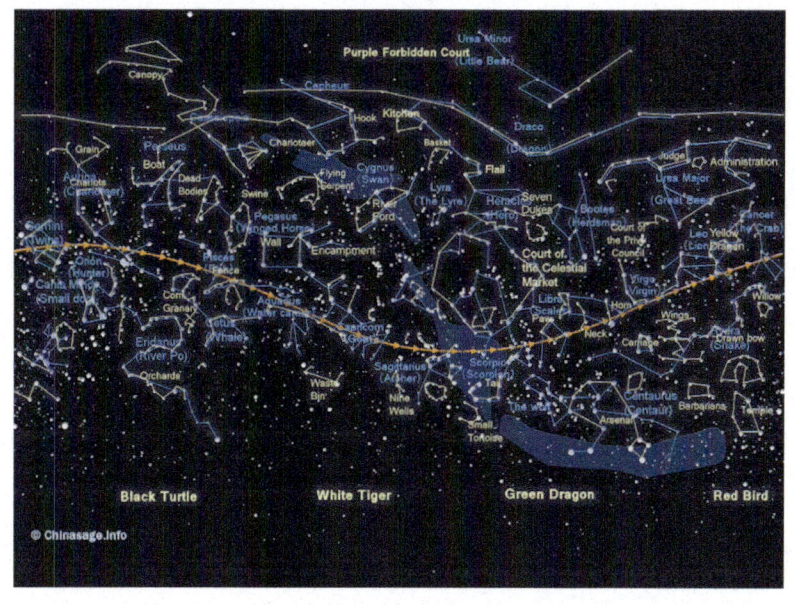

You may want to come back to this map as you read the descriptions below. It will (hopefully) make more sense after that. You should imagine this map as a circle, and it will come together better for you.

Sān yuan (Three Enclosures)

The central region of the sky was the most important as it was synonymous with the Emperor and therefore China itself. The Emperor is at the north celestial pole, the fixed point around which all other stars revolve. Laid out underneath him is a celestial landscape broadly reflecting the layout of an imagined Imperial court, organized by the Three Enclosures. Geographically the heavenly kingdom is centered beside a river, the Milky Way, just like China itself.

The following description summarizes the central region beautifully:

"The Three Enclosures are three institutions which compose the kingdom: the palace (Purple Forbidden Enclosure), the government complex (Supreme Enclosure), and the marketplace (Heavenly Market Enclosure).

The nomenclature of the stars in these enclosures are based on actual people and things that may be found in the market or the palace.

The emperor periodically rides out in his chariot (the moon) to survey his kingdom, just like on earth. Encircling the three enclosures are a set of 28 pitstops ("mansions") which the emperor visits on his survey. That's why all 28 mansions are located along the ecliptic path.

With respect to western constellations, the 28 mansions correspond to the zodiac, while the three enclosures correspond to the constellations enclosed by the ecliptic around the north celestial pole.

Each enclosure has two walls, a left wall (左垣) and a right wall (右垣), which roughly defines the area enclosed. The walls don't entirely connect, so the area is loosely defined in the same way that city walls define the extent of a city." Reddit user chris-ni

The middle region housed among its stars the celestial image of the Emperor surrounded by his family and civil and military officials. This part of the sky has constellations such as 'the prince', 'the concubine', and 'the throne' and reflects Chinese life on earth.

Purple Forbidden Enclosure (紫微垣, *Zǐ Wēi Yuán*): This is the area of the sky that directly reflects the Emperor's home on Earth. It occupies the north celestial pole area of the night sky. From the viewpoint of the ancient Chinese, the Purple Forbidden Enclosure lies in the middle of the sky and is circled by all the other stars. Stars and constellations of this group are visible all year from temperate latitudes in the Northern Hemisphere.

Supreme Palace Enclosure (太微垣, *Tài Wēi Yuán*): Stars and constellations of this group are visible during spring in the Northern Hemisphere (autumn in the Southern). It is in the general direction of vernal equinox.

Heavenly Market Enclosure (天市垣, *Tiān Shì Yuán*): Stars and constellations of this group are visible during late summer and early autumn in the Northern Hemisphere (late winter and early spring in the Southern). It is in the general direction of the Winter Solstice.

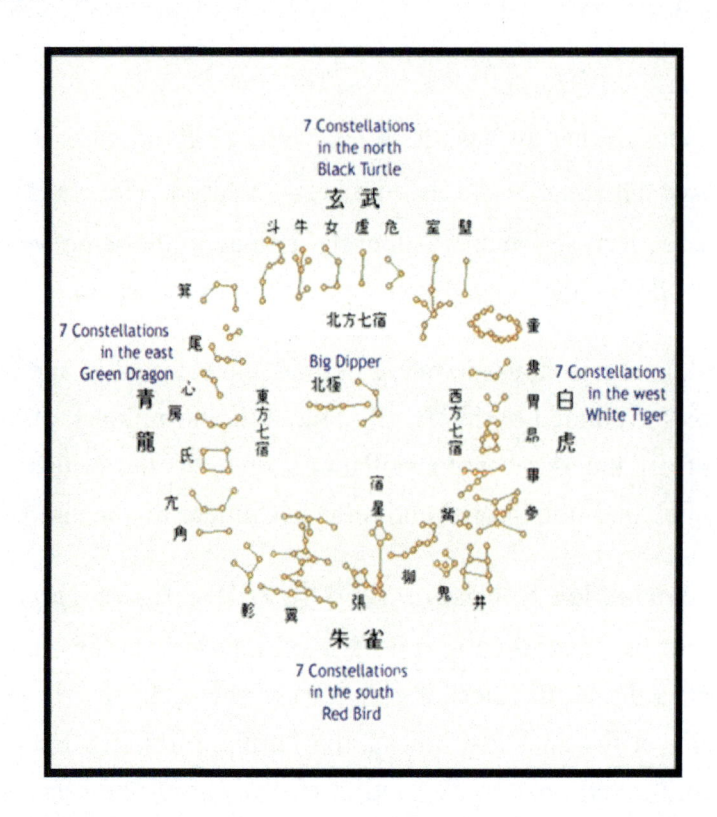

Shijin (Four Directions)

The *shijin*, or Four Symbols, are important mythological creatures in Taoism and feng shui. It is important to note that these four animals are entirely unrelated to the twelve animals of the Chinese zodiac. They have their own important associations and properties.

The Black Tortoise, *Xuan wu* (玄武) or Genbu, represents both North and the Winter.

A symbol of longevity, the tortoise of the north is often depicted together with a snake. Sometimes he is represented as two separate creatures and sometimes he is represented as a single tortoise/snake combo animal. The union of these two creatures was thought to have created the Earth. It is also associated with the element Water, the planet Mercury, and the color black. He represents the virtue of knowledge and controls the cold.

Genbu is the only one of the four directions that is not named after the animal it portrays. *Gen* means "dark or mysterious" and *bu* means "warrior". The reason that he is not "Black Tortoise" in the same pattern as the other animals is because the word 'tortoise' is also used as a slur in China. He is very important to the Taoist religion; the intertwining of the snake and tortoise is considered a symbol of lifelong fertility and the balance of yin and yang.

Greek Counterparts: The tortoise's shell is in Capricornus, Aquarius, and Pegasus. The snake's neck is in Sagittarius, and the ones which make up the snake's tail are in Pegasus and Andromeda.

The Azure Dragon, *Qing long* (青龙) represents both East and the Spring.

Unlike in western mythology, the dragon is rarely depicted as a malevolent force but generally considered to be both benevolent and auspicious. Although fearsome and powerful, they are equally considered just, benevolent, and the bringers of wealth and good fortune

He is associated with the element of wood, the season of Spring, the planet Jupiter, and the colors blue and green. He represents the virtue of benevolence and symbolizes creativity. He controls the rain. Represents the yang principle; often portrayed surrounded by water or clouds. In Chinese mythology, there are five types of dragons: (1) the celestial dragons who guard the abodes of the gods; (2) dragon spirits, who rule over wind and rain but can also cause flooding; (3) earth dragons, who cleanse the rivers and deepen the oceans; (4) treasure-guarding dragons; and (5) imperial dragons, those with five claws instead of the usual four.

Greek counterparts: The neck and head are in Virgo, the chest in Libra, the belly heart, and tail are in Scorpio, and his butt (winnowing basket) is in Sagittarius.

The Vermilion Bird, *Zhu que* **(朱雀)** represents both South and the Summer.

It is associated with the element of Fire, the planet Mars, and the color Red. He represents the virtue of propriety and controls heat and flame. said to have chicken's head, swallow's chin, snake's neck, fish's tail, and five-color feather. The bird is also sometimes seen as a phoenix. It is portrayed with radiant feathers, and an enchanting song; it only appears in times of good fortune. Believed to guide deceased souls to heaven and the symbol of a happy marriage.

Greek Counterparts: The left wing of the bird is in Gemini. His head feathers or comb is in Cancer. His head, beak, and body are in Hydra. His left wing is in Hydra and Crater. His tail feathers are in Corvus.

The White Tiger, *Bai hu*, (白虎) represents the West and the Autumn.

He is associated with the element of Metal, the planet Venus, and the color White. The tiger is often seen as a protector and was thought to guard over the armies of the emperor and protect the spirits of the dead. It is associated with the element metal. He represents the virtue of righteousness and controls the Wind. It is a symbol of force and army, and so many things entitled White Tiger in ancient China are related to military affairs. The male tiger was, among other things, the god of war, and in this capacity, it not only assisted the armies of the emperors, but fought the demons that threatened the dead in their graves. The White Tiger was seen as a protector and defender, not just from mortal enemies, but also from evil spirits and demons. He is therefore considered a symbol for bravery.

Greek Counterparts: The rear of the tiger is in Andromeda and Pisces. The middle of the tiger is in Aries and Taurus. His front legs and head are in Orion.

A view of the Chinese vision of the sky

Four Symbols; Pinyin; Planet; Element; Color	Mansion; Pinyin	Translation; Association	Greek Star
Azure Dragon of the East 东方苍龙 dōng fāng qīng lóng Spring Jupiter Wood Blue and Green	1) 角 Jiǎo 2) 亢 Kàng 3) 氐 Dǐ 4) 房 Fáng 5) 心 Xīn 6) 尾 Wěi 7) 箕 Jī	Horn; Earth dragon Neck; Sky dragon Root; Badger Room; Hare Heart; Fox Tail; Tiger Winnowing basket; Leopard	α Virgo κ Virgo α Libra π Scorpio σ Scorpio μ Scorpio γ Sagittarius
Black Tortoise of the North 北方玄武 běi fāng xuán wǔ Winter Mercury Water Black	8) 斗 Dǒu. 9) 牛 Niú 10) 女 Nǚ 11) 虚 Xū 12) 危 Wēi. 13) 室 Shì 14) 壁 Bì.	Southern dipper; Qilin Ox Girl; Bat Emptiness; Rat Rooftop; Swallow Encampment; Bear Wall; Porcupine	φ Sagittarius β Capricorn ε Aquarius β Aquarius α Aquarius α Pegasus γ Pegasus
White Tiger of the West 西方白虎 xī fāng bái hǔ Autumn/Fall Venus Metal White	15) 奎 Kuí 16) 娄 Lóu 17) 胃 Wèi 18) 昴 Mǎo 19) 毕 Bì 20) 觜 Zī 21) 参 Shēn	Legs; Wolf Bond; Dog Stomach; Pheasant Hairy head; Cockerel Net; Raven; Moon Turtle beak; Monkey Three stars; Ape	η Andromeda β Aries 35 Aries 17 Taurus ε Taurus λ Orion ζ Orion
Vermilion Bird of the South 南方朱雀 nán fāng zhū què Summer Mars Fire Red	22) 井 Jǐng 23) 鬼 Guǐ 24) 柳 Liǔ 25) 星 Xīng 26) 张 Zhāng 27) 翼 Yì 28) 轸 Zhěn	Well prop; Tapir Ghost; Sheep Willow; Deer Star; Horse Extended net; Deer Wings; Snake Chariot; Worm	μ Gemini θ Cancer δ Hydra α Hydra υ1 Hydra α Crater γ Corvus

Hopefully this illustration helps you visualize better how the 28 mansions are categorized and how they are named.

The Five Element Theory

Some ancient Chinese valued the Earth over the stars. These scientists looked for the reasons behind the natural order of things. They agreed that all things had a basis in one of Five elements: Fire, Earth, Metal, Water, or Wood. They examined how these basic elements worked together and against each other.

Five Element Theory asserts that the world changes according to the five elements *generating* or *overcoming* relationships. Generating and overcoming are the complementary processes — the yin and yang — of Five Element Theory. Generating processes *promote* development, while overcoming processes *restrain* development. By promoting and restraining, systems are harmonized, and balance is maintained. These visuals help illustrate this idea:

- **Water** (水 shui) is associated with the potential of new life hidden in the dark ground beneath the snows of winter.

- **Wood** (木 mu) is associated with the exuberance of new growth as it shoots up from the earth in the spring.

- **Fire** (火 ho) is associated with the process of maturation that takes place under the warmth of the summer sun.

- **Earth** (土 tu) is associated with ripening of grains in the yellow fields of late summer.

- **Metal** (金 jin) is associated with the harvest of autumn and the storage of seed for next year's planting and a new cycle.

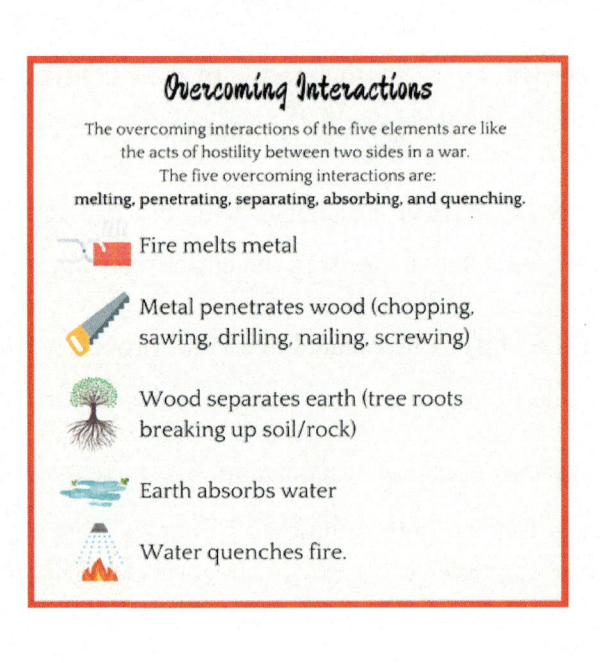

Generating Interactions

The generating interactions of the five elements are like the conception, gestation, birth, and nurture relationship between a mother and a baby. Such element pairs are deeply attached, and together imply success and luck.
The five generating interactions are
fueling, forming, containing, carrying, and feeding:

- Wood feeds a fire
- Fire makes ash (earth)
- Earth contains metal
- Metal holds water (as in a pail or bucket)
- Water breeds wood

Overcoming Interactions

The overcoming interactions of the five elements are like the acts of hostility between two sides in a war.
The five overcoming interactions are:
melting, penetrating, separating, absorbing, and quenching.

- Fire melts metal
- Metal penetrates wood (chopping, sawing, drilling, nailing, screwing)
- Wood separates earth (tree roots breaking up soil/rock)
- Earth absorbs water
- Water quenches fire.

Five Elements Theory and the Chinese Zodiac

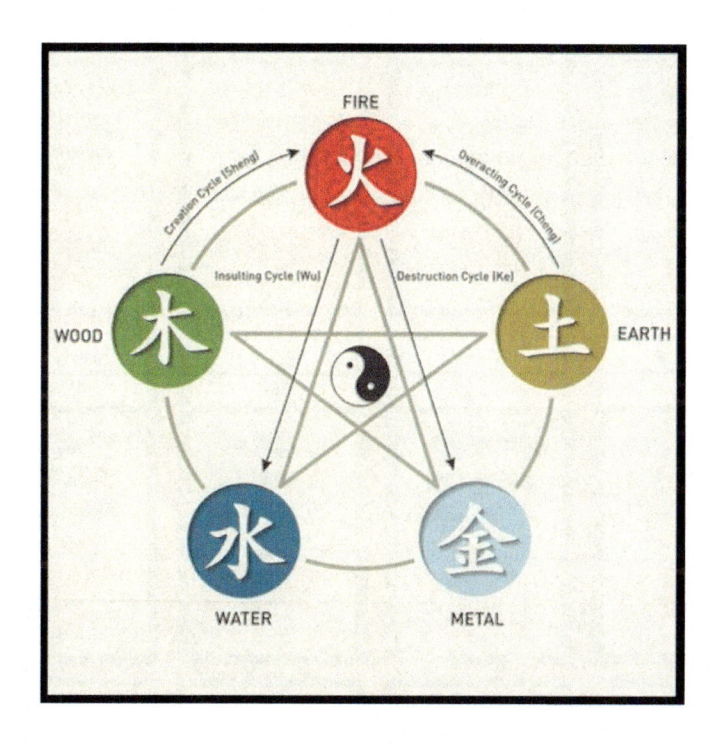

Let's take another look at that Zodiac chart from the beginning of the book in case you want a refresher at this point as to which Element you are. Remember this is based on the 60-year cycle we learned about in the last section. The element you are, mixed with your Zodiac animal, adds a nuance of almost tactile character to your animal sign. Then we will dive into Element descriptions.

What is your Chinese Zodiac Sign?

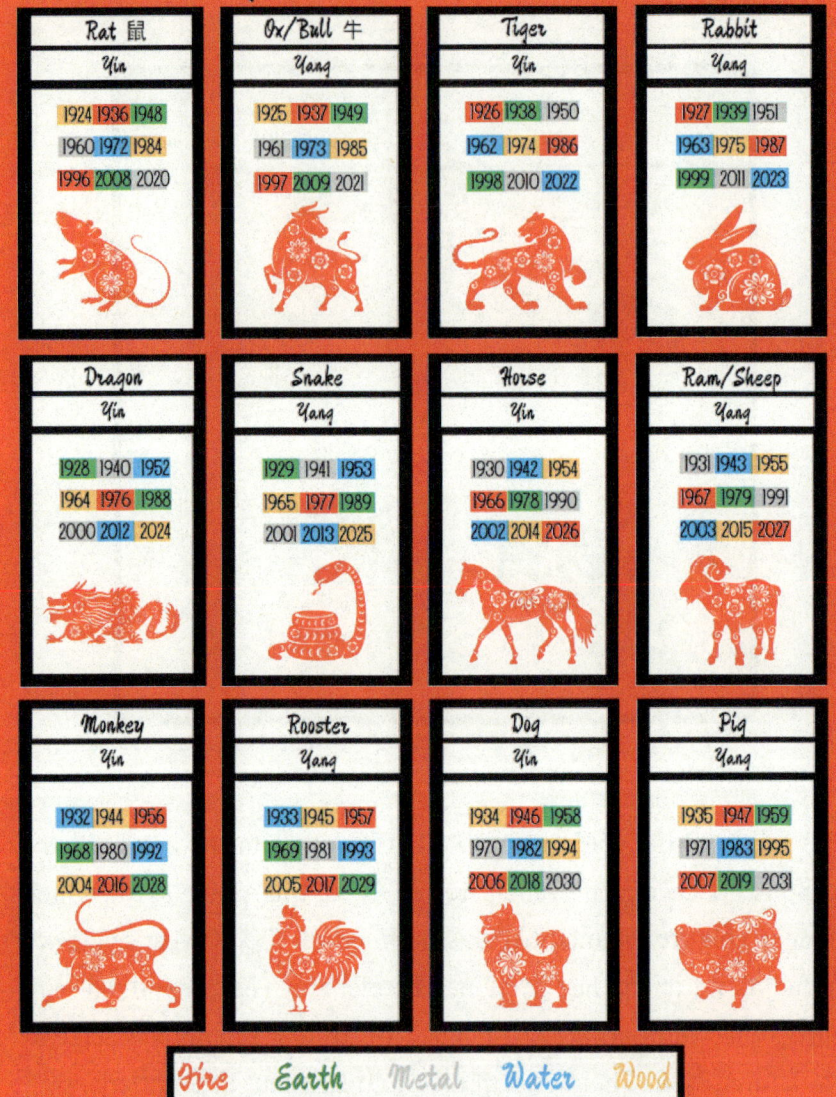

Rat 鼠 Yin	Ox/Bull 牛 Yang	Tiger Yin	Rabbit Yang
1924 1936 1948 1960 1972 1984 1996 2008 2020	1925 1937 1949 1961 1973 1985 1997 2009 2021	1926 1938 1950 1962 1974 1986 1998 2010 2022	1927 1939 1951 1963 1975 1987 1999 2011 2023

Dragon Yin	Snake Yang	Horse Yin	Ram/Sheep Yang
1928 1940 1952 1964 1976 1988 2000 2012 2024	1929 1941 1953 1965 1977 1989 2001 2013 2025	1930 1942 1954 1966 1978 1990 2002 2014 2026	1931 1943 1955 1967 1979 1991 2003 2015 2027

Monkey Yin	Rooster Yang	Dog Yin	Pig Yang
1932 1944 1956 1968 1980 1992 2004 2016 2028	1933 1945 1957 1969 1981 1993 2005 2017 2029	1934 1946 1958 1970 1982 1994 2006 2018 2030	1935 1947 1959 1971 1983 1995 2007 2019 2031

Fire   Earth   Metal   Water   Wood

Traits of the Element Metal

Those born in years of the Chinese calendar ending in either 'zero' or 'one' are said to have the element of Metal.

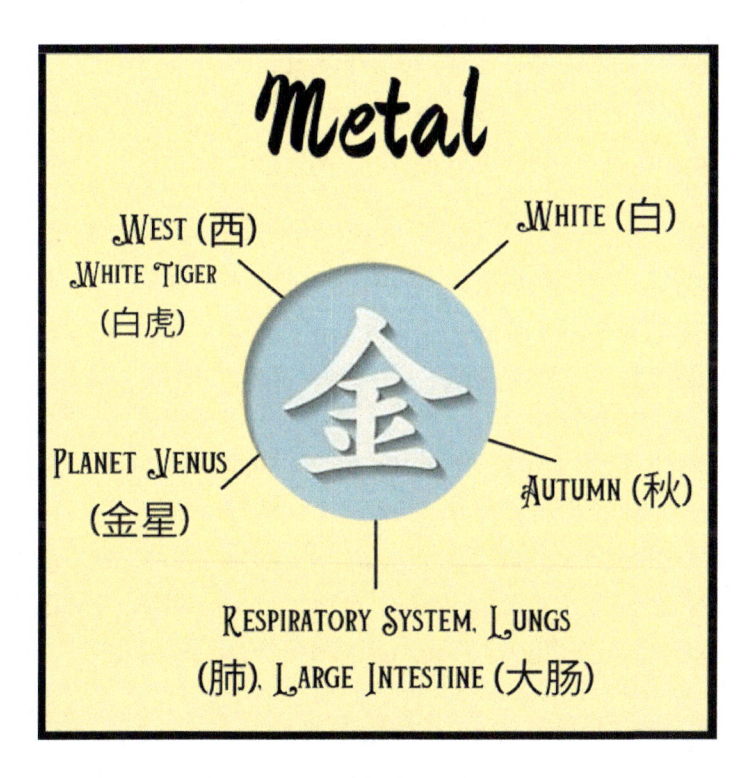

Metal

- West (西)
- White Tiger (白虎)
- Planet Venus (金星)
- 金
- White (白)
- Autumn (秋)
- Respiratory System, Lungs (肺), Large Intestine (大肠)

Metal people enjoy the finer things in life. Fine wine, rich chocolates, the sweetness of true love: all spark the heart and imagination of those born to metal.

Personal space and time for reflection are equally important to those with the metal element. Beautiful scents, flowers and scenery will ease the emotions and feed the soul's need for the romantic.

Metal people are on a high spiritual path. They have the greatest respect for that path and will seek out those who can teach them to reach the next spiritual level.

Those with a Metal element are typically sentimental and kind. They will go out of their way to help you. They approach life with perseverance, emotional strength, and unyielding determination. A Metal person knows their goals and will not stop until those goals are met.

Metal people are self-reliant, sometimes to a fault. They can be viewed as aloof and unconcerned with others. That self-reliance needs another one of Metal's ear marks: organization and stability.

Metal people need to pay attention to the state of their emotions, as they are considered prone to depression and suicide. The personal reflection mentioned earlier is very important for this aspect as well. Nurturing relationships and continually challenging themselves to be better versions of themselves is also key.

Metal people should decorate their homes with things that are beautiful to them to help maintain internal and emotional balance,

Metal governs the lungs. Those with the metal element may be more likely to suffer diseases of the lungs such as asthma.

Famous Metal people: Angelina Jolie, Victoria Beckham

Traits of the Element Water

Those born in years of the Chinese calendar ending in either 'two' or 'three' are said to have the element of Water.

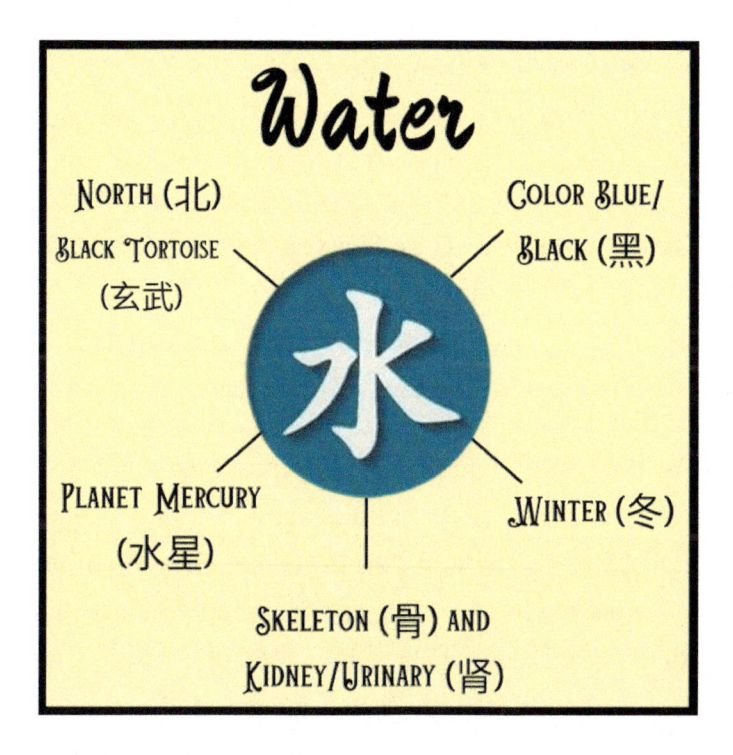

Water

- North (北)
- Black Tortoise (玄武)
- Planet Mercury (水星)
- Color Blue/Black (黑)
- Winter (冬)
- Skeleton (骨) and Kidney/Urinary (肾)

Water is a necessary component for the survival of any species on Earth. Without this life force, crops wither and die. Both water itself and the food it helps grow are vital. Yet, with too much water, death occurs. Floods, over-watering of crops or ourselves: over-abundance is indeed a curse. Water is ripe with contradictions.

Water is the only element with the ability to put out fire and make things grow and thrive. It is a delicate balance that all life must adhere to. It is for this very reason the element water is represented by the color black.

Water rules intelligence and wisdom. People born under the element Water are uncommonly intelligent and capable. Diplomatic, and intuitive, water people are flexible. They have a special ability to "go with the flow" and are usually laid-back.

Water people are those who dive deep into all life has to offer. They EXPERIENCE life. They feel the rain drops and notice the smell of the raindrops; they deeply contemplate art or a beautiful piece of music. They do not want to hurry through life, and this shows in their walk, talk, and the way they react.

Those with the water element make friends easily and do well in social situations. They are charming and compassionate. These traits, coupled with the natural flair for communication of the water sign, means those with this element are good leaders, and make good partners. Waters everywhere love lounging with good friends and waxing eloquently about all that is right and wrong with the world.

Sometimes Water people go TOO deep into the rights and wrongs of reality and themselves, and this leads them to become depressed. Everything starts to look distorted, like if you went into a swimming pool and opened your eyes. They can need help getting themselves out of this mindset.

For all their wisdom and reasoning ability, Water people tend to have difficulty making and sticking to decisions. They tend to over-analyze the situation and examine it from all sides and angles over and over. This leads to anxiety and an inability to make up their mind. This overwhelms with details means that Water people have trouble seeing an idea through.

It is said that Water rules the Excretory system and has rule over the kidneys. Those with the water element should exercise caution with all things pertaining to their kidneys.

Famous Water people: Kurt Cobain, Nicolas Cage

Traits of the Element of Wood

Those born in years of the Chinese calendar ending in either four or five, are said to have the element of Metal.

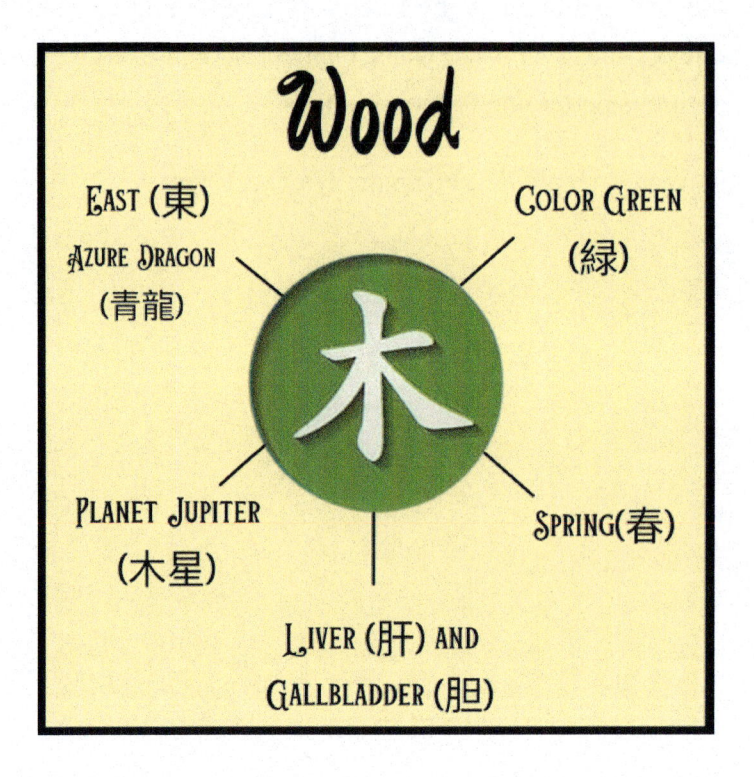

```
                    Wood
  East (東)                        Color Green
  Azure Dragon                        (綠)
   (青龍)
                      木
  Planet Jupiter
    (木星)                         Spring (春)

                Liver (肝) and
                Gallbladder (胆)
```

The element of Wood represents the direction East. Those who are born with this element tend to yearn for stability and tradition.

In China, wood is also associated with bamboo. Bamboo, of course, is a strong, flexible, and long shoot which grows in marsh areas. It follows then, that Wood people are flexible, emotionally strong, and dependable. A Wood person will stick with you through good and bad times, unwavering in their support.

Wood people are interested in social issues and strive to leave the poor and helpless of our world with a sense of independence and change. Although, they can be idealistic, and that trait can be the cause of emotional angst when plans don't follow the perfect path.

Wood people are very fair-minded and hate injustice. They do well in social work or working with children.

Working with others is easy for wood people, as they truly enjoy the process of cooperation and compromise. They enjoy learning and thrive in social situations. Wood people do not do well as hermits or loners, lack of interaction with other people will lead to unhappiness. However, they are honest to a fault, and this can make them seem harsh. They love debates and arguments, and it will take a solid argument to sway their opinion.

Like trees, Wood people seek to expand their roots. Think of tree roots coming up out of solid concrete and you get a feel for how determined a Wood person can be. They are doers and turn ideas into action. Woods exude confidence and don't let much stand in their way. They know what they want, are decisive, make things happen, and push themselves to the limit.

Spring is the season of Wood, and it represents growth and newness. Represented by browns and greens, spring is the season when life begins and flourishes. The same is said of those with the Wood element. They are sensual and can see the beauty in everyday situations.

Generous and warm, Wood people spread happiness, confidence, and joy wherever they go. However, wood also carries with it anger. Wood people are prone to temper that can ruin their relationships if they aren't careful. It helps Woods to have an upbeat partner who frequently gives them a pat on the back or a high-five. A quick acknowledgement lets Woods know that their hard work is acknowledged by the people they want to please the most.

In the body, wood element rules the liver and gall bladder. Yin people must take great care to keep the liver in top condition, for this is their weak point. Those with Yang orientation, the gall bladder is the point of concern.

Famous Wood people: Simon Cowell, Pink

Traits of the Element Fire

Those born in years of the Chinese calendar ending in either six or seven, are said to have the element of Fire.

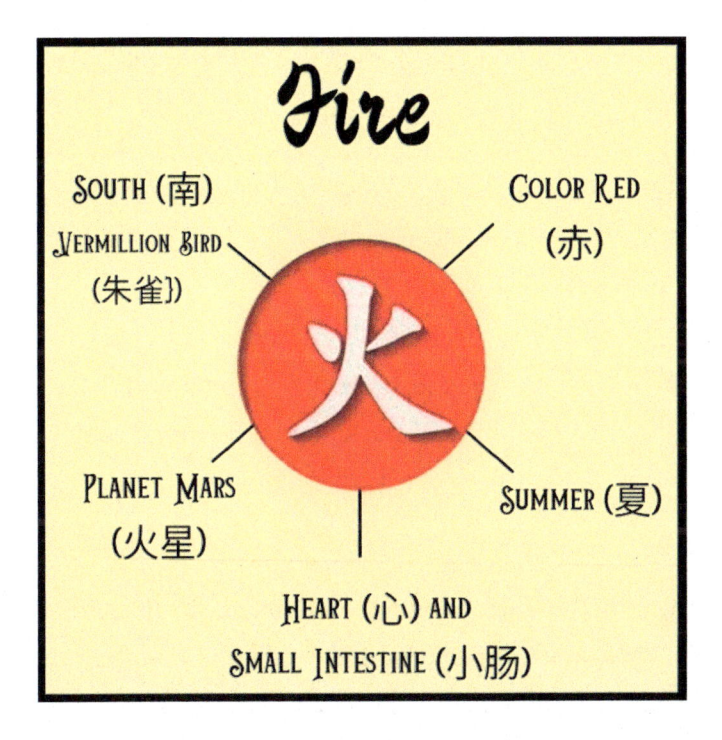

Fire

- South (南)
- Vermillion Bird (朱雀)
- Color Red (赤)
- Planet Mars (火星)
- Summer (夏)
- Heart (心) and Small Intestine (小肠)

Fire is both destructive and nourishing. On a cold winter day, there is nothing more calming to the soul than curling up by a roaring fire with a good book or cherished loved one. On the other side, there is no other force on earth more destructive than a raging, out of control fire. A mixed bag indeed!

Those under the influence of Fire have charm and magnetism on their side. They draw attention to themselves and have an infectious enthusiasm that makes them natural leaders. People just can't help but to follow them because managing others comes so naturally. They take the role of leader seriously and do it well. They are understanding yet firm, decisive, and compassionate.

Fire people have a natural joy about life that is infectious; they can bring others out of depression, darkness, and boredom. They find seemingly mundane situations to be filled with wonder and excitement: life is a party, and they are here for it!

Fire people make excellent entrepreneurs. They possess the determination, drive and plain stubbornness needed to make a new endeavor thrive in today's tough business world. Fire people have an innate ability to see through all the confusing distractions right to heart of the matter. They possess the strength and determination to successfully navigate themselves and their team through any and all obstacles. What they can't finesse around, they will burn though.

Those born to the Fire element tend to be restless. They need excitement and innovation to be happy. While their infectious joy and enthusiasm make them "everyone's best friend", they find relationships difficult because Fire often lacks the stability needed to sustain close relationships. When faced with displeasure from others, a Fire's joy can turn to panic.

Fire rules the circulatory system and the heart, making these top areas of concern. Fire people should take special care to maintain these systems. Healthy diets and dedicated exercise time helps keep them from becoming an out of control, destructive mess. Relaxing hobbies to stay in touch with their creativity prevents stress from building up.

Famous Fire people: Jim Carrey, Ellen Degeneres,

Traits of the Element Earth

Those born in years of the Chinese calendar ending in either eight or nine, are said to have the element of Metal.

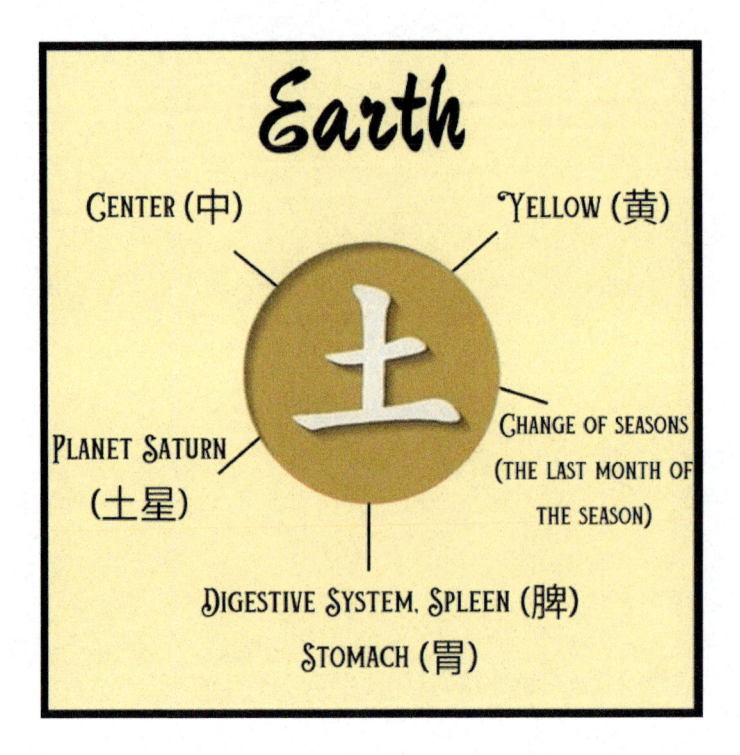

Earth

- CENTER (中)
- YELLOW (黄)
- PLANET SATURN (土星)
- CHANGE OF SEASONS (THE LAST MONTH OF THE SEASON)
- DIGESTIVE SYSTEM, SPLEEN (脾)
- STOMACH (胃)

Unlike the position of the Earth in our solar system, the element of earth lies dead center in the Chinese astrological charts. This is because ancients believed the Earth was the center of the universe and all celestial bodies circled our planet.

People born under the element of Earth seem to feel the universe revolves around them as well. Ambitious and stubborn, Earth people are used to getting what they want and achieving their goals. Failure is foreign to them. They are skilled at looking at a situation and evaluating what is needed.

Goals are achieved through hard work and determination. Earth people know how to plan for the long term, and they are stable enough to stick with the plan to its completion.

The stubbornness of the Earth element is definitely a double-edged sword. It gives those born under its rule the determination to follow through when things are tough; it also gives the audacity to defend their point even when they are wrong. For Earth people, the past is comfortable, and change can be excruciating.

Earth as an inviting, bountiful caretaker (Mother Earth anyone?) also defines those born under this element. Compassion and caring are their trademarks.

Being the center of the universe doesn't mean you are self-centered! The Earth element handles the charge of caretaker with grace and ease. Earth people are patient and thoughtful and take the time to care for those around them. In fact, they learn skills (cooking, sewing, painting etc.) simply to be able to give hand-made gifts to those around them.

Those under this element enjoy service work and are likely to take on jobs where they are helping others. Good Earth element jobs include nurses, doctors, teachers, and therapists. They want to make you feel comfortable, safe, and to know you are loved. They want to give to the whole world, and very often have children as the ultimate gift back to mankind.

Deep inside, they are hoping for love in return. When Earth people don't get love in return, they fall into ugly co-dependent cycles that never seem to end.

Those with the Earth element tend to have difficulties with the stomach and spleen. Careful attention to diet is very important, as is chewing food carefully. Anything an Earth person can do to enhance digestion will be a great aid to maintaining optimal health.

Famous Earth people: Mr. Rogers, Pope Francis

The 12 Signs of the Zodiac

In this section we will dive deep into each of the 12 Signs of the Chinese Zodiac. While there is no basis in fact with these descriptions, there is fun to be had in seeing how well we match up to these descriptions...or not!

Let's start with this delightful story behind how the order of the 12 animals was chosen. Some details fluctuate with the telling, but the overall story remains the same. The BBC wrote this version so well, it has been copied in full here:

"The story goes that a race was organized by the Jade Emperor - one of the most important gods in traditional Chinese religion - who invited all the animals in the world to take part.

Only twelve species turned up at the start line: a pig, dog, rooster, monkey, sheep, horse, snake, dragon, rabbit, tiger, ox, and rat.

As a reward for turning up, the Emperor named a year in the zodiac after each one, while the race would determine the order each animal would be placed.

The course included a huge river which every creature, large or small, had to cross.

The exhausted rat used its cunning to navigate the water by persuading the kindly ox to let it sit on its head as it crossed. Rather than say thank you on the other side, the rat made a dash for the finish with the ox not far behind.

That's why the rat is first creature in the cycle, followed by the ox.

Not surprisingly, the tiger ran a good race but the current in the river sent it a little off course. It recovered enough to cross the line behind the ox and so comes in at number three in the Chinese zodiac.

Next up was the rabbit. Tired by the race, it almost became a cropper [failure] in the river but saved itself on a floating log and got to shore to finish fourth.

In fifth place is the only mythical creature on the calendar, the dragon. A kinder creature than legend suggests, it didn't hesitate to divert from the race to extinguish a fire which was endangering the lives of some nearby villagers. Once it got back on course, it saw the rabbit struggling and used its breath to blow it safely to shore.

The rabbit never learned who came to its aid while the dragon was content to finish behind it.

The horse wasn't far behind the dragon and thought sixth place was in the bag. However, it hadn't noticed that the snake was saving energy by wrapping itself around the horse's leg to hitch a ride. With the finish line in sight, the snake uncoiled itself and frightened the horse enough to slither into sixth, leaving its carrier, the horse, to take seventh place.

Next up were the sheep, monkey, and rooster and this is a perfect example of teamwork.

The three piloted a small raft which would see them across the river safely.

Once on the other side it was a dash for the finish. The sheep was first, followed by the monkey and then the rooster (in some parts of the world, the sheep is known as a goat), so they took slots eight, nine and ten respectively.

Now we're just left with the dog and the pig. Dog owners won't be surprised that the playful hound was more interested in splashing about in the river rather than crossing it. This enabled the first 10 creatures to overtake it. It eventually ran over the line in 11th place.

Which leaves the pig.

The pig got peckish during the race. After stopping for food, it became sleepy and dozed off. It did wake up after a while and managed to make it over the line in last place. The Emperor had almost given up on it but was happy to assign it the final space in the zodiac.

Why isn't there a Year of the Cat? So prevalent in Chinese culture (who doesn't love a lucky waving cat?), why you may ask does the feline not feature in the zodiac? Well, that's down to the rat.

Although the pair were friends, the cat asked the rat to wake it up for the race as it had a habit of sleeping in. The rat was so excited, it forgot. By the time the cat woke up, it was far too late to enter. Hopefully, their friendship survived this most bitter of hiccups."

The traits and compatibility of these animals is up next!

First, let's look at the special relationships the Zodiac signs have with each other. This is not to say that relationships outside of these listed are not worthy of pursuing, but rather that these are simply very beneficial to all involved.

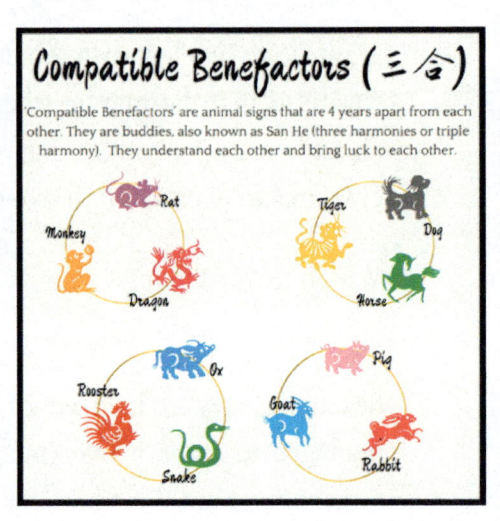

Secret Benefactors (六合)

'Secret Benefactors' are akin to a guardian angel, more potent than the compatible groups. The six pairs of Secret Benefactors are set according to the combination of Yin and Yang. Known as **Liu He** (six harmonies), it is the species that helps you. The two animals in the same group get along well and give each other great help, either publicly or in secret, no matter in their love life or career.

- Pig & Tiger
- Dragon & Rooster
- Snake & Dog
- Horse & Ram
- Rat & Ox
- Rabbit & Monkey

Compatible Benefactors (三合)

'Compatible Benefactors' are animal signs that are 4 years apart from each other. They are buddies, also known as San He (three harmonies or triple harmony). They understand each other and bring luck to each other.

- Monkey, Rat, Dragon
- Tiger, Horse, Dog
- Rooster, Ox, Snake
- Pig, Goat, Rabbit

With all this background and context, let's dive into each specific Zodiac sign!

Rat

Rat Year	Lunar Zodiac Year	Element
2020	Jan. 25, 2020 – Feb. 11, 2021	Metal
2008	Feb. 7, 2008 – Jan. 25, 2009	Earth
1996	Feb. 19, 1996 – Feb. 6, 1997	Fire
1984	Feb. 2, 1984 – Feb. 19, 1985	Wood
1972	Feb. 15, 1972 – Feb. 2, 1973	Water
1960	Jan. 28, 1960 – Feb. 14, 1961	Metal
1948	Feb. 10, 1948 – Jan. 28, 1949	Earth
1936	Jan. 24, 1936 – Feb. 10, 1937	Fire
1924	Feb. 5, 1924 – Jan. 23, 1925	Wood

Use this chart to confirm you are the Rat based on the Lunar New Year dates.

The Rat is the first sign of the Chinese Zodiac. As we saw in the story, the rat used cunning and manipulation to win the race.

In Chinese astrology, some of the signs have names that we in Western culture might not associate with positive human characteristics. Chief among these might be the sign of the Rat.

While in the West, we associate rats with sewers, vermin and disease, this animal is viewed a bit differently in the East. The Eastern rat is appreciated for its quick wits and ability to accumulate and hold on to wealth. Rats are a symbol of good luck in the East.

The ancients considered the rat to be a protector. It was thought to bring material wealthy and prosperity. Aggression, charm, death, wealth, pestilence, order, war, and the occult were all ruled by the rat.

Rats enjoy being on the outside looking in, as they like to learn by observing. They're forever observant, always tucking away information in their brains for use at some future time if they need it. Rats don't like to be bored and are always looking for challenges to keep their already-sharp wits even sharper.

Organized and intelligent, Rat people are said to be leaders who value that power. They are strong-willed and ambitious and tend to adapt easily to new situations and environments. They are practical and hardworking and have tight control over their emotions.

Rats are fair in business and become injured when others are not. They are usually quick-tempered and vengeful. They will not think twice about seeking revenge when they, or someone they love, is wronged.

Passionate and charming, Rats make friends easily and tend to choose friends carefully. Their sharp tongue and quick wits make them great debaters, and they do love to debate! Rats do not trust easily but are fiercely loyal to those few who manage to win their trust. Sometimes, however, that loyalty can get them in trouble.

However, as charming as they may be on the outside, Rat people are also known to be cold and calculating. Sometimes they may even be cruel if that is what is needed to reach their goal or promote their personal agenda. This Sign's charm and powers of persuasion are often used to their best advantage.

Those born under the sign of the Rat will do well to learn patience and tolerance with others AND themselves.

Rat people tend to be perfectionists and easily become obsessed with the minor, often unimportant details of daily life. In order to build their sense of self and worth, time spent in relaxation is important.

You are most compatible with Dragons and Monkeys and least compatible with Horses.

OX

牛

Ox Year	Lunar Zodiac Year	Element
2021	Feb. 12, 2021–Jan. 31, 2022	Metal
2009	Jan. 26, 2009 – Feb. 13, 2010	Earth
1997	Feb. 7, 1997 – Jan. 28, 1998	Fire
1985	Feb. 20, 1985 – Feb. 9, 1986	Wood
1973	Feb. 3, 1973 – Jan. 22, 1974	Water
1961	Feb. 15, 1961–Feb. 5, 1962	Metal
1949	Jan. 29, 1949–Feb. 16, 1950	Earth
1937	Feb. 11, 1937–Jan. 30, 1938	Fire
1925	Jan. 24, 1925–Feb. 12, 1926	Wood

Use this chart to confirm you are the Ox based on the Lunar New Year dates.

The Ox is the second sign in the Chinese Zodiac. Like the animal they are named after, Ox people tend to be powerful and steady. Oxen were traditionally used to plow fields and haul heavy loads. They make good work animals because of their dependable and patient attitudes. Ox people have these same qualities.

The Ox is the sign of prosperity through fortitude and hard work. This powerful sign is a born leader, being quite dependable and possessing an innate ability to achieve great things. As one might guess, such people are reliable, calm, and modest. Like their animal namesake, the Ox is unswervingly patient, tireless in their work, and capable of enduring any amount of hardship without complaint.

Ox people need peace and quiet to work through their ideas and feelings. When they have set their mind on something it is hard for them to be convinced otherwise (in other words, bull-headed).

An Ox Person has a very logical mind and is extremely systematic in whatever they do, often to the point of lacking creativity. They are methodical and do not plunge in without considering what the right steps are to get a project finished. They believe in doing it right the first time and prefer logic and reasoning over emotional appeals.

Ox people speak little but are extremely intelligent and bright. When necessary, they are articulate and eloquent. They prefer to lead and don't like to be pushed around and can be rather dogmatic in their dealings.

Ox people are truthful and sincere, and the idea of wheeling and dealing in a competitive world is distasteful to them. They are rarely driven by the prospect of financial gain.

These people are always welcome because of their honesty and patience. They have many friends who appreciate the fact that the Ox people are wary of new trends, although every now and then they can be encouraged to try something new. Their dependability makes them a patient and inspiring friend. Oxen make outstanding parents.

While the Ox has many admirable qualities, it can also be a bit judgmental. This characteristic can keep them from having the close friends and relationships that they desire. Some good advice for the Ox is to learn to value qualities in others, and to listen to what others have to say. Sometimes it pays to simply say nothing.

The Ox is not extravagant. The thought of living off credit cards or being in debt makes them nervous. Likewise, the possibility of taking a serious risk could cause the Ox sleepless nights.

It is important to remember that the Ox people are sociable and relaxed when they feel secure, but occasionally a dark cloud looms over them. The weight of the whole world's problems gets them down, and they seek solutions for those problems.

Ox should marry a Snake or Rooster, though can certainly be content by themselves. Avoid those Sheep/Rams.

Tiger

Tiger Year	Lunar Zodiac Year	Element
2022	Feb. 1, 2022 – Jan. 21, 2023	Water
2010	Feb. 14, 2010 – Feb. 2, 2011	Metal
1998	Jan. 28, 1998 – Feb. 15, 1999	Earth
1986	Feb. 9, 1986 – Jan. 28, 1987	Fire
1974	Jan. 23, 1974 – Feb. 10, 1975	Wood
1962	Feb. 5, 1962 – Jan. 24, 1963	Water
1950	Feb. 17, 1950 – Feb. 5, 1951	Metal
1938	Jan. 31, 1938 – Feb. 18, 1939	Earth
1926	Feb. 13, 1926 – Feb. 1, 1927	Fire

Use this chart to confirm you are the Tiger based on the Lunar New Year dates.

The third sign of the Chinese Zodiac is the Tiger. In the Eastern world, it is the Tiger who is considered the king of beasts, as opposed the lion of the West. In keeping with the sovereignty of the Tiger, those who carry this sign are respected and feared. They are said to bring with them power, good fortune and an air of royalty. Many believe powerful Emperors will be reincarnated under the sign of the Tiger.

Tiger is definitely king. Noble and warm-hearted, Tigers have a natural, raw appeal that's extremely attractive to other Signs. Tiger people typically have magnetic personalities, and they usually assume an air of authority. Other people are drawn to the energy and natural leadership of the Tiger.

They're not just about attraction, though. Tigers will fight the good fight to the bitter end if the cause is deemed worthy. Opponents are wise to fear this feline. Tigers will face most situations with confidence and grace, even when leading others into dangerous or uncertain circumstances.

Tigers are courageous and fearsome beyond compare. They generally come out ahead in battle, be it in the boardroom or the bedroom. Seduction is one area where the Tiger is King.

On the other hand, Tiger people are calm, gentle mysterious and soft. They are fiercely loyal, and tend to have long-lasting, stable friendships, even as those relationships rock with the moods of the Tiger.

The Tiger has a potent natural ability that is often in great danger of being abused. They can be vain, quarrelsome, and overly aggressive at times, but their inherent charisma and vast reserves of charm are usually sufficient to extract them from any problems that may arise from their lack of foresight.

A lesson that Tigers would be well-served to learn is moderation in all things. Once these cats can find their center and direct their considerable energies toward worthwhile endeavors (as opposed to racing through life), they will accomplish much.

Enthusiastic, determined and optimistic, Tigers are often admired by those who know them. Tigers are very secure with themselves and their decisions. They are comfortable following their instincts and enjoy the unpredictable.

Tigers thrive in a business atmosphere and do well to start their own business. Tigers enjoy doing things themselves and thrive under the pressure of new, exciting experiences. They face the unusual or difficult with unwavering confidence. They can be aggressive in pursuit of their goals.

Those born under the tiger are usually straightforward, open, and honest. They do not respond well to feeling trapped, emotionally speaking. In this situation a Tiger will either withdraw completely or will become aggressive and attack the person trying to corner him. Once they calm and recover their confidence and security, the Tiger will return to the situation and try again.

In general, the Tiger is a sound partner, and a reliable friend. Having Tiger in your life will assure that life is never boring. Look to the Horse and Dog for happiness. Beware of the Monkey.

Rabbit

兔

Rabbit Year	Lunar Zodiac Year	Element
2023	Jan. 22, 2023–Feb 9, 2024	Water
2011	Feb. 3, 2011–Jan 22, 2012	Metal
1999	Feb. 16, 1999–Feb 4, 2000	Earth
1987	Jan. 29, 1987–Feb 16, 1988	Fire
1975	Feb. 11, 1975–Jan 30, 1976	Wood
1963	Jan. 25, 1963–Feb 12, 1964	Water
1951	Feb. 6, 1951–Jan 26, 1952	Metal
1939	Feb. 19, 1939–Feb 7, 1940	Earth
1927	Feb 2, 1927–Jan 22, 1928	Fire

Use this chart to confirm you are the Rabbit based on the Lunar New Year dates.

In the Fourth position of the Chinese Zodiac is the Rabbit. Rabbits are one of the more emotional and sensitive signs. Rabbits are the caretakers of the Chinese Zodiac and enjoy caring for those around them. They make great listeners and are usually the confidante of many.

Timid and attractive, the Rabbits of the Chinese Zodiac tend to act more like bunnies, whether they like it or not! This Sign is extremely popular and has a wide circle of family and friends. It's compassionate nature leads it to be very protective of those it holds dear.

However, where romance is concerned, the Rabbit's sentimentality can lead it to idealize relationships. The sweet, sensitive Rabbit often ends up giving more of itself to a partner than is realistic or healthy. The good news is, when this Sign goes off-balance, the Rabbit's core group of friends and its stable home life help bring it back to center.

The Rabbit is a rather delicate Sign that needs a solid base to thrive. Lacking close, supportive friends and family, the Rabbit might just break down in tears at the first sign of conflict. Emotional upsets in this Sign's life can even lead to physical illnesses.

Rabbits dislike arguments and other conflict and will try anything to avoid a fight; this results in something of a pushover nature. However, when they are passionate about something a rabbit will step out of her den and show the strong, confident, and unwavering side of her nature.

Rabbits can lapse into pessimism and may seem "stuck" in life; this is often done to mask their insecure natures. Rabbits tend to move through life's lessons at their own contemplative pace. It's a waste of time to become exasperated with this Sign's seeming disinterest in facing it's problems and conquering them.

With the right partner -- meaning someone whose high principles won't allow it to take advantage of this sensitive, giving Sign -- the Rabbit can make an incredibly loving and protective partner or family member. Rabbits love to entertain at home and always make sure their house is comfortable and tastefully furnished.

Those born under the sign of Rabbit have a natural ability when it comes to decorating and entertaining. They have an eye for color and interior design and are wonderfully adept when it comes to planning the minute details of a beautiful event. They always know the perfect place to put that couch, and the perfect thing to say. Rabbit people are patient and slow to anger.

What Rabbits need most is a stronger sense of self-worth and the security that comes with it. Their discerning natures, coupled with some hard-won assertiveness, will help these happy creatures go far.

Thoughtful and personable, Rabbits are ideally suited to serve as politicians, ambassadors, or diplomats. Rabbits also fit in well in the world of culture and high society. They are well-mannered and enjoy the finer things in life.

Because of their sensitive nature, Rabbits get along well with many people. However, in the depths of their hearts, they are reserved and usually prefer to spend their time quietly engrossed in intellectual pursuits.

The gentle nature of those born under the Rabbit make them timid and anxious. They are not risk takers. A rabbit much prefers the routine and known to the unknown They will almost always choose the safe route. Sometimes this will lead the Rabbit to miss or pass up new experiences or a good opportunity.

The most compatible match for a Rabbit is the Goat or the Pig.

Dragon

Dragon Year	Lunar Zodiac Year	Element
2024	Feb 10, 2024–Jan 28, 2025	Wood
2012	Jan 23, 2012–Feb 9, 2013	Water
2000	Feb 5, 2000–Jan 23, 2001	Metal
1988	Feb 17, 1988–Feb 5, 1989	Earth
1976	Jan 31, 1976–Feb 17, 1977	Fire
1964	Feb 13, 1964–Feb 1, 1965	Wood
1952	Jan 27, 1952–Feb 13, 1953	Water
1940	Feb 8, 1940–Jan 26, 1941	Metal
1928	Jan 23, 1928–Feb 9, 1929	Earth

Use this chart to confirm you are the Dragon based on the Lunar New Year dates.

The Dragon is the only mythical creature in the Chinese Zodiac. As a symbol, the dragon holds a special place in Chinese culture. Dragons are placed on roofs and above doors to bring strength, health, luck, and harmony to the inhabitants. Dragons are said to ward off evil spirits and banish demons to the underworld.

The Dragon is traditionally associated with the position of Emperor of China, and because of that is felt to be omnipotent. Chinese parents are so eager to have a Dragon baby, they will intentionally plan for one. The hospitals are overrun with parents in this year, and infant mortality rate goes up!

The Dragon is one of the most powerful and lucky Signs of the Chinese Zodiac. It's warm heart tempers its fiery and rambunctious nature. This is a giving, intelligent and tenacious Sign that knows exactly what it wants and is determined to get it.

Dragons possess a certain natural charm that ensures they can always influence their peers. They often find themselves the center of attention in social situations. Their charismatic and dominant personalities make them natural CEOs, start-up founders, politicians, and military commanders. This Sign is truly blessed, too. Dragons are considered to be very lucky in love. The Dragon's friends are always keen to hear what this firebrand has to say. When it comes to dispensing advice, the Dragon has the floor. The Dragon is a steadfast friend, offering unwavering support in times of great need. With a Dragon by your side, you will never feel abandoned.

Dragons lean toward the grandiose in all things. Whether it's money, food, luxury, passion, or power, for the Dragon, enough is never enough. Dragon people like to do things BIG. They are intelligent and when they learn to combine their talents, intelligence and overwhelming energy, the dragon has no problem fulfilling his often overly ambitious goals. But along with this tendency toward indulgence, the Dragon possesses the ability to learn, manage and blend the positive and negative traits of this sign.

Its ego can get in the way, but even so, this larger-than-life creature has a knack for creativity and leadership. According to Dragons, it's their natural born right to lead the way -- because who else could do it so surely and so well? They make solid leaders, too, knowing instinctively what needs to be done to stay on top.

Crossing the Dragon is never a good idea -- this beast can singe. A valuable life lesson for this clever creature would be to absorb the principles of flexibility, compassion, and tolerance. Being high and mighty can serve to inspire others, but it also keeps Dragons from living their lives to the fullest. If Dragons can learn to balance their quest for success with an appreciation for the little things, their life will be more than worthwhile.

As lucky as they are, Dragons have a good chance of achieving considerable material wealth during their lifetimes, although it isn't mere money that is this Sign's main motivation. Power is what the Dragon wants and truly believes it deserves. Dragons are quite the opportunists, forever searching for ways in which to consolidate their considerable power.

Contrary to all this strength and fire, a weakened Dragon is a sad sack, a creature that refuses to take defeat with even a modicum of grace. They tend towards the negative. This negativity, if left unchecked, will drive people away in droves.

Dragons can come across as ego-centric, rude, arrogant, and ill-tempered. Jealousy is the Dragon's enemy. They must be ever watchful against the tendency to use deceit and plain nastiness against one they feel has wronged them.

The most compatible match for a Dragon is the Monkey or the Rat.

A couple of famous western individuals born under the sign of the dragon are Martin Luther King Jr., Vladimir Putin, Che Guevara, Bruce Lee, Salvador Dali, and John Lennon.

Snake

蛇

Snake Year	Lunar Zodiac Year	Element
2025	Jan. 29. 2025 – Feb. 16. 2026	Wood
2013	Feb. 10. 2013 – Jan. 30. 2014	Water
2001	Jan. 24. 2001 – Feb. 11. 2002	Metal
1989	Feb. 6. 1989 – Jan. 26. 1990	Earth
1977	Feb. 18. 1977 – Feb. 6. 1978	Fire
1965	Feb. 2. 1965 – Jan. 20. 1966	Wood
1953	Feb. 14. 1953 – Feb. 3. 1954	Water
1941	Jan. 27. 1941 – Feb. 14. 1942	Metal
1929	Feb. 10. 1929 – Jan. 29. 1930	Earth

Use this chart to confirm you are the Snake based on the Lunar New Year dates.

The sixth house of the Chinese Zodiac is the Snake. Snakes are traditionally considered the wisest and most mysterious of all the signs. They are a bundle of contradictions. They are wise and intense with a tendency towards physical beauty. Also considered vain and high-tempered.

The Snake is an interesting mix of extroversion paired with introversion; intuitive reasoning paired with business savoir-faire. Snakes are lucky with money and will generally have more than enough to live life to the fullest, regardless of how important it considers money to be; this may be due to the fact that Snakes tend to be rather tight with cash. They're not stingy; they're simply more active mentally than physically.

Snakes tend to hang back a bit to analyze a situation before jumping into it. Their charming, seductive quality belies a rather retiring nature; this Sign is perfectly happy to spend the whole day curled up with a good book and thus, can be mislabeled as being lazy.

The Snake is somewhat insecure deep down and tend to be a rather jealous and possessive lover. This behavior can end up alienating loved ones.

Despite these less-than-stellar tendencies, however, the Snake often proves irresistible and is a generous, loving partner. Slightly dangerous and disarmingly smart, the Snake's philosophical and intuitive mind generally supersedes logic in favor of feelings and instinct.

Snake people are natural communicators and enjoy stimulating and varied conversations. They easily become bored by everyday discussions. To keep the attention of a snake, you must find interesting, new, or cutting-edge things to talk about. Once you lose their attention, there is no getting it back.

Snakes will rely on their own gut reactions and intuitions before turning to others for suggestions and are gifted at evaluating a situation. They can easily see the underlying nuances of any situation and they use their innate wisdom to evaluate and make judgments. These qualities make this Sign a great hand in any business venture. They are also wonderfully suited to work in the financial realm. A snake would thrive on Wall Street.

Snake people are born problem-solvers and while they will listen with empathy and openness to the ideas and opinions of others, they are not influenced by those opinions. Snake people make up their own minds and stick to their guns.

Sometimes, however, this strong sense of confidence gets the snake into trouble. They are not good at taking advice, even when they know they need it. This causes the snake to make mistakes they could have avoided simply by hearing the experiences of those they trust.

Ever watchful for the new and unusual, the Snake will be the first person to embrace a new idea or technology. They love the finer things in life: a good book, superb meal, extraordinary music. However, snakes have no patience for activities they view as foolish or frivolous.

They also find happiness studying religion, philosophy, or psychology. They do not do well in repetitive or boring jobs.

In general Snakes are generous and genteel, charming, and appealing. Snake people are good friends and good citizens. They believe in helping where they are needed and are patient teachers.

Snakes must try to learn humility and to develop a stronger sense of self. Once Snakes realize that confidence comes from within, they will finally be comfortable in their own skin.

The most compatible match for a Snake is the Rooster or the Ox.

Horse

马

Horse Year	Lunar Zodiac Year	Element
2026	Feb. 17, 2026-Feb. 5, 2027	Fire
2014	Jan. 31, 2014-Feb. 18, 2015	Wood
2002	Feb. 12, 2002-Jan. 31, 2003	Water
1990	Jan. 27, 1990-Feb. 14, 1991	Metal
1978	Feb. 7, 1978-Jan. 27, 1979	Earth
1966	Jan. 21, 1966-Feb. 8, 1967	Fire
1954	Feb. 3, 1954-Jan. 23, 1955	Wood
19412	Feb 15, 1942-Feb. 3, 1943	Water
1930	Jan. 29, 1930-Feb 16, 1931	Metal

Use this chart to confirm you are the Horse based on the Lunar New Year dates.

The seventh house of the Chinese Zodiac is the Horse. Like a wild mustang, horse people are said to be independent, and confident. They tend to be free spirits who need ample space to run free. They intensely dislike feeling confined or penned up. They're popular and attractive to the opposite sex.

Horse people are the life of the party and center of attention...and they love every minute of it! This Sign possesses a sharp wit and a scintillating presence; it really knows how to work a crowd. Love connections tend to come easily to Horses, since they exude the kind of raw sex appeal that is a magnet to others. This Sign tends to come on very strong in the beginning of the relationship, having an almost innate sense of romance and seduction. Horses are seducers in general; check out any A-list party and you're bound to find the Horse in attendance.

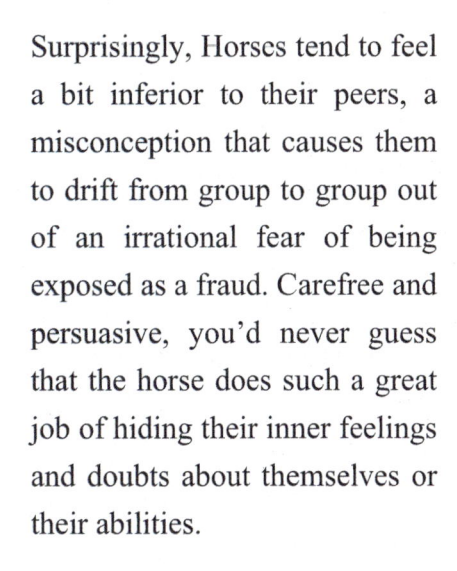

Surprisingly, Horses tend to feel a bit inferior to their peers, a misconception that causes them to drift from group to group out of an irrational fear of being exposed as a fraud. Carefree and persuasive, you'd never guess that the horse does such a great job of hiding their inner feelings and doubts about themselves or their abilities.

Horses are the nomads of the Chinese Zodiac, roaming from one place or project to the next. All this Sign's incessant activity and searching may be to satisfy a deep-rooted desire to fit in. Horses crave love and intimacy, which is a double-edged sword since it often leads them to feel trapped. Once they find some peace within themselves, they can curb their wandering tendencies and learn to appreciate what's in their own backyard.

Do you have an innovative new idea? Go find horse person to share it with. They will be the first to tell you how wonderful it is. And they're excitement will help spur you into action. Who knows, maybe some of their wonderful horse wisdom and advice will give you a start on making your idea a reality!

All this energy, enthusiasm, and spontaneity can lead the horse astray. They are prone to jumping from one great idea to the next, without finishing much, and tend to not look much at the big picture. They just follow their whims, which can result in a trail of prematurely ended relationships, jobs, projects and so on.

Horse people are good at thinking on their feet. This tendency to be quick-witted combined with natural horse sense means prosperity, luck and happiness are the horse's pasture.

Giving, attentive and good listeners, horse people make great friends and partners. They are gentle with the thoughts and feelings of others.

Although, horse people tend to get excited and aren't very good at keeping secrets. They don't mean to betray trust; their enthusiasm just gets the best of them.

Horses are known for their honesty and determination. They know how to set a short-term goal and achieve it. Known for being intelligent, most horse people will tell you they are cunning, not smart. They're great with numbers and have a natural aptitude for recognizing patterns.

Also, those born under the sign of the horse will do very well to avoid those who carry the sign of the Rat. It could lead to explosive results. They should marry a Tiger or a Dog.

Goat 羊

Goat Year	Lunar Zodiac Year	Element
2027	Feb. 6, 2027–Jan. 25, 2028	Fire
2015	Feb. 19, 2015–Feb. 7, 2016	Wood
2003	Feb. 1, 2003–Jan. 21, 2004	Water
1991	Feb. 15, 1991–Feb. 4, 1992	Metal
1979	Jan. 28, 1979–Feb. 15, 1980	Earth
1967	Feb. 9, 1967–Jan. 29, 1968	Fire
1955	Jan. 24, 1955–Feb. 12, 1956	Wood
1943	Feb. 4, 1943–Jan. 24, 1944	Water
1931	Feb 17, 1931–Feb. 5, 1932	Metal

Use this chart to confirm you are the Goat (Sheep/Ram) based on the Lunar New Year dates.

Eight in the circle of Chinese Astrology is the Sheep. Some cultures refer to this sign as the Ram or Goat. Whichever you call them, people born to this sign are creative, interesting, and emotionally sensitive. They are elegant, creative, somewhat timid and prefer anonymity.

Goats tend to have a hard time with romance. Anyone who couples up with a Goat must know that this Sign has a sensitive streak a mile wide and can be subject to bouts of anxiety over seemingly inconsequential things. Goats need plenty of love, support, and open reassurance from their lovers. If a relationship is marked by conflict, the Goat will often pull away -- either physically or simply by retreating into the haven of its imagination.

If the romance is going well, however, Goats won't hesitate to tell their partner what they need -- and they can be quite insistent about it. This Sign will return the favor, however; the Goat has a luxurious side that delights in indulging a lover's every wish. Appearances are also important to the Goat, which may explain why these folks can spend hours primping and posing.

Goats are generally most comfortable in their own minds (which other, more linear-thinking Signs may have trouble deciphering).

This Sign makes a great craftsperson or artisan-- any occupation that allows its mind the full range of freedom.

Goats tend not to be very well-organized, precluding many more dry business endeavors. In fact, Goats tend not to be very materialistic in general, finding plenty of riches in their own imagination. However, especially when in love, the Goat can be quite a lavish gift-giver.

Sheep have a flair for the artistic. Their innate sense of drama and rhythm make them great actors and musicians. In fact, almost the entire list of "famous Sheep" is comprised of well-known actors, cartoonists, and musicians. These are beautiful people, who enjoy creating beautiful things. On the same token, Sheep people need to surround themselves with beautiful things. They cannot function when their environment is in disarray or just plain ugly.

Sheep are considerate and respectful They will never dream of intentionally hurting your feelings and being sneaky or manipulative is against their very nature. If a Sheep injures in any way, they will quickly step up and do all within their power to make amends.

The Sheep can be needy and dependent. They need the approval of their family and friends and can sometimes demand a lot of reassurance.

Sensitive and loving,

Sheep oftentimes have trouble coping with the harsh realities of our modern world. They cry while watching the news and ache for the crime or war victim. It doesn't matter that they have never met this person, or if they are half a world away: the pain and level of caring is the same as if it were themselves or their best friend.

Sheep tend to avoid confrontation. Tense situations pull at their natural love of all things. Sheep thrive when they feel protected and loved.

Sheep people should gift themselves with a career or hobby in the creative arts. Painting or fashion design, or crafting will provide a terrific outlet for all that wonderful Sheep energy.

You are most compatible with Pigs and Rabbits, but don't mix it up with the Ox.

Monkey

Pig Year	Lunar Zodiac Year	Element
2028	Jan. 26. 2028 – Feb. 12. 2029	Earth
2015	Feb. 19. 2015 – Feb 7. 2016	Fire
2004	Jan. 22. 2004 – Feb 8. 2005	Wood
1992	Feb. 4. 1992 – Jan 22. 1993	Water
1980	Feb. 16. 1980 – Feb. 4. 1981	Metal
1968	Jan. 30. 1968 – Feb. 16. 1969	Earth
1956	Feb. 12. 1956 – Jan. 30. 1957	Fire
1944	Jan. 25. 1944 – Feb. 13. 1945	Wood
1932	Feb. 6. 1932 – Jan. 25. 1933	Water

Use this chart to confirm you are the Monkey based on the Lunar New Year dates.

The ninth position on the Chinese Zodiac is held by the ever-contradictory Monkey. The monkey is known across China for honesty, justice, sorrow, and adultery. At the same time, the symbol of the Monkey is worshipped as a "Great Sage, Equal with Heaven".

They are described as intelligent and able to influence people. An enthusiastic achiever, they are easily discouraged and confused.

Monkeys are good listeners and tackle complicated situations with ease. This Sign's natural curiosity gives it a broad-based intellectual curiosity. Monkeys have a show-off side that loves nothing more than to impress their friends with all they know.

The Monkey's world, full of reckless energy and revelry, isn't for everyone. Remember, though, it's not that this Sign is mean; it might just be a bit too curious for its own good. Monkeys often feel the need to try everything at least once, which can make for a merry-go-round of relationships.

The Monkey's love of self-indulgence can also lead to other types of trouble. This Sign may have limited self-control concerning food, alcohol, and other pleasurable activities. It's party time all the time for the Monkey, yet when it leads to a monster hangover or a shattered heart (generally someone else's, not theirs), this Sign might show a touch of remorse. They won't flat-out admit the error of their ways, but at least they'll pull back and try to tone things down -- for a while.

Monkeys must try to learn to think of others ahead of themselves, at least some of the time. This Sign's world will be more complete once it realizes the world doesn't revolve around it.

Honesty and trust are the top features of this sign. You can trust a Monkey person with your deepest, darkest secrets and those secrets will go to the grave with your Monkey. In business, your money, ideas, and the very company itself is well-protected in the hands of the reliable Monkey.

People born under the sign of the Monkey are especially adept when it comes to taking stock of a situation and making good snap decisions. And the Monkey person always knows what's going around her. She can hear and absorb information from others' conversations, making that emergency decision even easier.

Of course, the flip side is that the Monkey remembers everything you ever say to them. That can come back to bite you later.

Intelligence, quick thinking, creative genius makes this sign well suited inventing new ways of doing things and new items. Of course, monkeys are good at creating trouble, too.

This combination of traits also means the Monkey will hold you accountable if you commit a wrong against them. Their reputation is very important to them, and they will not stop until they even the score. To outsiders, this tends to make them look like master manipulators, but really, they're not.

The monkey is usually content with themselves and their lives. They have morals, but they tend to change with the circumstances. This usually has the tendency to make a mess of things, but in true monkey form, the monkey person doesn't stick around long enough to help clean up the mess.

Your best matches are with a Dragon or a Rat; beware the Tiger.

Rooster

Rooster Year	Lunar Zodiac Year	Element
2029	Feb. 12, 2029–Feb. 2, 2030	Earth
2017	Jan. 28, 2017–Feb. 16, 2018	Fire
2005	Feb. 9, 2005–Jan. 28, 2006	Wood
1993	Jan. 23, 1993–Feb. 9, 1994	Water
1981	Feb. 5, 1981–Jan. 24, 1982	Metal
1969	Feb. 17, 1969–Feb. 5, 1970	Earth
1957	Jan. 30, 1957–Feb. 17, 1958	Fire
1945	Feb. 13, 1945–Jan. 31, 1946	Wood
1933	Jan. 26, 1933–Feb. 13, 1934	Water

Use this chart to confirm you are the Rooster based on the Lunar New Year dates.

The tenth sign in the circle of Chinese astrological chart is the Rooster. Like the reputation of its namesake, people born under this sign are usually pretentious and conceited. The Rooster is described as a pioneer in spirit, devoted to work and the quest for knowledge. It is selfish and eccentric

Roosters are quick thinkers and are practical and resourceful, preferring to stick to what is tried and true rather than taking unnecessary risks. Roosters are keen observers of their surroundings and those around them. It's hard to slip anything past a Rooster since they seem to have eyes in the backs of their heads. This quality can lead others to think the Rooster is psychic, but that's not generally the case. Instead, this Sign enjoys a keen attention to detail that makes it a whiz at anything requiring close analysis.

Roosters tend to be perfectionists and expect to be in control, especially over their appearance. Primping and posing for the Rooster can go on forever. Being noticed and admired is an aphrodisiac for Roosters, and they can go a long time on a few kind words. Roosters also adore being out on the town, especially if they're in the company of adoring friends. The Rooster will also be the best-dressed one of the bunch -- style counts with this Sign, regardless of the cost.

Roosters are almost always preoccupied with their looks. You will never find a rooster with a hair out place, and they are always perfectly dressed. They are attractive, and they like to dress to impress. Those born to the rooster will be the first to notice when you wear a new outfit. And, when they say you look stunning, they mean it. On the other hand, they are just as likely to notice and comment when you're not looking your best.

Roosters need to learn to value their heart and soul as much as their good looks. Their excellent people skills and sharp minds are qualities that others will appreciate as much as a pretty face. For all this preoccupation with looks, the rooster is equally hard on himself. "You're your own worst critic" describes the rooster perfectly.

Roosters love to be in the middle of everything. They truly shine when all attention is on them. Throwing a dinner party for fifty of their closest friends is fun and relaxing for them. Don't forget to bring along a friend or two, as well. Roosters love meeting and impressing new people. They thrive on the unexpected.

Roosters are typically straight-forward in their dealings with other people. You can always count on them to give an honest opinion- sometimes to a fault. Their lack of tact can leave others feeling hurt and offended, although that is not generally the rooster's intention.

On the other side, rooster people are wise, and compassionate. They are confident in their opinions and judgments. Brave and willing to help, roosters are good people to have on your side during a row of bad luck.

Attention to detail is their strong point. Roosters revel in the opportunity to show off their skills with small details. They make great lawyers, brain surgeons and accountants, to name a few of this Sign's possible occupations. Above all else, the Rooster is very straightforward and rewards others' honesty in kind.

Roosters are best matched with Snakes and Oxen.

Dog 狗

Dog Year	Lunar Zodiac Year	Element
2030	Feb. 3, 2030- Jan. 22, 2031	Metal
2018	Feb. 15, 2018-Feb. 4, 2019	Earth
2006	Jan. 27, 2006-Feb. 17, 2007	Fire
1994	Feb. 10, 1994-Jan. 30, 1995	Wood
1982	Jan. 25, 1982-Feb. 13, 1983	Water
1970	Feb. 6, 1970-Jan. 26, 1971	Metal
1958	Feb. 18, 1958-Feb. 7, 1959	Earth
1946	Feb 1, 1946-Jan. 21, 1947	Fire
1934	Feb. 14, 1934-Feb. 3, 1935	Wood

Use this chart to confirm you are the Dog based on the Lunar New Year dates.

Loyal to a fault, the dog is the eleventh sign of the Chinese Zodiac. Dogs are faithful, honest, and always stick to their firm codes of ethics. Oftentimes, this makes them intolerant of those who show weakness. Dogs do not accept weakness in themselves, either. They are generally quite trustworthy, except for the occasional little white lies the Dog tells to make things go more smoothly.

The Dog makes a wonderful, loyal friend and is an excellent listener. This Sign tends to root for the underdog and its keen sense of right and wrong makes it duty-bound to the core. To be born under Dog influence is to be an idealist. Dog people have a very clear idea of right and wrong, there is very little room in their heart for shades of grey. The Dog's motto seems to be: "Live right, look out for the little people and fight injustice whenever possible."

Dogs don't go in for light social banter; instead, they go straight for home, discoursing on the topics that are most important to them. At these times the Dog's narrow-minded or stubborn side can become apparent; this Sign has trouble staying light and calm when an important issue is at stake. Dog people tend to come across to others as excessively critical, even picky. The dog will see every flaw, and their sense of propriety will not allow them to over-look even the smallest flaws. They are perfectionists.

The Dog's discerning nature makes it an excellent businessperson, one who can turn that picky, guarded nature into a keen sense of the truth of another's motives. Dog people are usually cool headed in a crisis. They are the ones you can count on during hectic, stressful times. Honest, strong, intelligent, and practical, Dogs will accept whatever fate throws at them and handle it with poise and grace. You can count on people of the dog to do their work thoroughly and well.

Dog people will stand by their family and friends...even when maybe they shouldn't. Sensitive and compassionate, those with the Dog sign empathize with the pain you feel. They take it as if it were their own. This can lead the dog to make excuses for those who are less than respectful toward them. Dogs will also meddle in your personal life, in the name of trying to help. They mean well and most Dogs will understand when you suggest they back off.

This Sign can also be very temperamental; mood swings characterize its emotional life and often the Dog needs to run off to be alone to recuperate. Part of the problem is the result of this Sign's load of irrational fears that turn into niggling anxieties that then turn into hurt feelings and grouchiness. This sensitive Sign needs to warm up to others over time and gradually learn to trust them. Without that trust as a foundation, Dogs can be judgmental and coarse.

Where love is concerned, Dogs often have a tough time finding the right match. Dogs need to work on controlling their irrational worries and would also be well-served to relax their mile-high standards, which can sometimes wind up alienating the ones they love. Dog people will do whatever it takes to protect their family and friends; they are unselfish, and only want the best for those they care about. Those with the dog sign will do well for themselves if they choose friends carefully and remember that not everyone deserves their steadfast loyalty.

The most compatible match for a Dog is the Tiger or the Horse.

Pig

猪

Pig Year	Lunar Zodiac Year	Element
2031	Jan. 22, 2031 – Feb. 10, 2032	Metal
2019	Feb. 4, 2019 – Jan. 24, 2020	Earth
2007	Feb. 17, 2007 – Feb. 6, 2008	Fire
1995	Jan. 30, 1995 – Feb. 18, 1996	Wood
1983	Feb. 13, 1983 – Feb. 1, 1984	Water
1971	Jan. 27, 1971 – Feb. 14, 1972	Metal
1959	Feb. 8, 1959 – Jan. 27, 1960	Earth
1947	Jan. 22, 1947 – Feb. 9, 1948	Fire
1935	Feb. 4, 1935 – Jan. 23, 1936	Wood

Use this chart to confirm you are the Pig based on the Lunar New Year dates.

The last symbol in the circle of Chinese Astrology is the Pig. In Western culture, this sign is often renamed the Boar to avoid any negative association with some of the slang definitions of the word 'pig'. Trustworthy, dependable, peaceful, and reserved: these are the cornerstone traits of the Pig.

Quiet and introspective, Pig people are at home with nature. They would much rather go for a quiet hike than hang out at the mall. At the same time, they prefer to be homebodies. They feel secure close to home and do not like taking risks or exploring new territory.

The Pig may be the most generous and honorable Sign of the Chinese Zodiac. Pigs are nice to a fault and possess impeccable manners and taste. They can be perceived as snobs, but this is a misconception; they are simply possessed of a truly luxurious nature. Pigs believe in the best qualities of mankind and certainly doesn't consider itself to be superior. This sign delights in finery and nice things: in surroundings, food, lovemaking, and otherwise.

Pigs also care a great deal about friends and family and work hard to keep everyone in their life happy. Helping others is a true pleasure for the Pig, who feels best when everyone else is smiling. A Pig with no one around to appreciate its giving nature is a sad thing indeed. Pigs are so magnanimous they can appear almost saintly; this can lead some less-than-well-intentioned souls to stomp all over this Sign, and the bad news is, the Pig will take the blows.

People born under the sign of the pig are quiet and reserved, usually shy. Pigs are content to work behind the scenes, away from the limelight and they typically do not seek credit or recognition. To strangers a pig person will come across disinterested and aloof. They make acquaintances easily, and usually seem to have many friends.

However, true friendship is a matter that must be closely guarded. You must earn the trust of the pig to be granted the honor of close friendship. They share their feelings with precious few. Once you have won the trust of a pig, you will find them to be open and giving. They cherish their friends and enjoy finding ways to show how much they care. Their natural honest and dependable nature allows others to trust them easily, and they would never even dream of breaking that trust.

Pigs are highly intelligent creatures, forever studying, playing, and probing in their quest for greater knowledge. They can be misinterpreted as being lazy, however, due to their love of reveling in the good stuff; this Sign could happily spend hours on end making love, napping, taking a long bubble bath or dallying over an incredible spread of rich foods.

Pig people are very concerned with what is socially acceptable. They are not trendsetters, preferring instead to follow rather than lead. Reflective in nature, Pigs will withdraw from a problem or disagreement to consider the situation. When they return, it will be with an eye to solving the problem to make both parties happy.

Pigs tend to make wonderful life partners due to their hearts of gold and their love of family. Even so, Pigs can be rather exclusive, choosing to spend time with those who will appreciate them most and ignore the rest of the populace. Pigs would do well to realize that there's more to life than being needed. When they open up their world to a diverse group of people, they will truly bloom.

The most compatible match for a Pig is the Rabbit or the Goat.

Credits:

https://mydaolabs.com/blogs/the-way/embracing-chinese-medicine-s-five-elements-in-a-western-diet

https://www.chinahighlights.com/travelguide/chinese-zodiac/five-lements-character-destiny-analysis-rat.htm

https://en.wikipedia.org/wiki/Twenty-Eight_Mansions

https://www.chinesefortunecalendar.com/CLC/LunarCalendar.htm

https://www.chinesefortunecalendar.com/AllCalendars.htm

https://knowinsiders.com/lunar-calendar-2021-moon-phases-2021-chinese-calendar-in-full-detail-27390.html

https://en.wikipedia.org/wiki/Chinese_astrology

https://www.chinasage.info/stars.htm#

https://www.yourchineseastrology.com/calendar/heavenly-stems-earthly-branches.htm

https://www.onmarkproductions.com/html/ssu-ling.shtml

https://thoth-adan.com/blog/five-heavenly-beasts

https://www.viewofchina.com/ancient-chinese-cosmology/

http://ancientchinaastronomy.weebly.com/constellations--discoveries.html

https://www.bbc.co.uk/bitesize/articles/zd9nd6f

https://en.wikipedia.org/wiki/Heavenly_Stems

http://tibetanbuddhistencyclopedia.com/en/index.php/Heavenly_Stems_&_Earthly_Branches

https://yokai.com/genbu/

http://idp.bl.uk/4DCGI/education/astronomy/sky.html

http://chinese-astrology.blogspot.com/2005/08/heavenly-stem-and-earthly-branch.html

https://www.bbc.co.uk/bitesize/articles/zd9nd6f

Sôma, Mitsuru; Kawabata, Kin-aki; Tanikawa, Kiyotaka (25 October 2004). "Units of Time in Ancient China and Japan". *Publications of the Astronomical Society of Japan*. **56** (5): 887–904.

陳浩新. 「冷在三九，熱在三伏」 [Cold is in the Three Nines, heat is in the Three Fu]. *Educational Resources – Hong Kong Observatory* (in Chinese). Archived from the original on 15 June 2018. Retrieved 15 May 2018.

Printed in Great Britain
by Amazon